The Shining *Eyes* of *Dawn*

MARILYN SMITH-HAWKINS

Quantum
Discovery
A LITERARY AGENCY

ISBN
978-1-961601-09-3(Paperback)
978-1-961601-10-9(eBook)

The Shining Eyes
of Dawn

Table of Contents

Dawn, three months old

Dawn, 2 years old

Dawn, 5 years old

Dawn, 11 years old

Dawn, 15 years old

Foreword

I was very pleased when Marilyn Smith asked me to write the foreword for this book, for doing so brings again to my mind one of the most delightful patients I have known, Dawn Marie Smith.

Dawn became a patient when she was found to have a brain tumor at the age of nine in 1975. She went through surgery, radiation, and the side effects of a ravaging disease with the quiet spirit and gentle poise that was very rare, even for an adult. It is a *terrible* task for a surgeon to see a patient in pain during the course of an illness such as a brain tumor. It is also heartbreaking to watch a young girl endure the changes in growth, development, and future plans as compared to her peers during adolescence when she must cope with a life-threatening and, eventually, life-taking disease.

Dawn was truly exceptional in her ability to always muster a smile, even through physical and emotional pain. Her family also was a rare gift to the medical team caring for Dawn, with their unflagging trust, faith, and positive attitudes.

It was an honor for me to be able to care for Dawn as her neurosurgeon and develop a relationship with her and her family, which surpassed the professional association to become one of feeling truly part of her family. This was what made her death so personally painful.

Those who knew her cannot forget her. Although Dawn's illness ended with her death in 1982, it is impossible for me to think of Dawn without seeing a smile, as I remember her never being without a smile for me.

Therefore, it is with great pleasure that I write this foreword to Dawn's story.

– Vicente C. Gracias, MD

Looking Back

It was a cold, gray morning when Dave and I drove from Wayland to Butterworth Hospital in Grand Rapids, Michigan. Normally, it was a thirty- minute drive, but on this day it seemed longer. Our daughter, Dawn, lay asleep in her hospital room, awaiting a day that would change all our lives. Both Dave and I felt a lot of pressure as we entered Dawn's room on the eleventh day of March 1975 at 6:30 a.m. Dawn looked so beautiful lying there asleep. I worried about what this day could mean to her.

Awakening when she felt our presence, she looked at us and cried, "Don't let them hurt me!" My heart went out to her, because I knew she had been through much already. Dave and I tried desperately to comfort her without much success. I didn't think we could again say, "It will soon be over." We had said that so many times in the past few weeks, and the end didn't seem any nearer. Over the previous three months she had been back and forth to the hospital three different times for tests. First of which was seven days of testing for stomach problems. She cried because those tests included drinking chulking tasting liquids several times for x-rays. Second time back was another six days because she started showing coordination problems. Third time back was testing the brain because she showed signs of double vision which led to the discovery of her tumor.

I felt torn as I looked into her crying eyes. I wanted to protect her. But how could I when I didn't understand what was going to happen to her that day? The nurse soon came in to give Dawn her pre-op shot. Dawn screamed violently, "No! No! No! I don't want any more!" I could hardly hold back the tears as Dave and I tried to give her some last-minute comfort. Dawn had every reason to cry and scream. After all, she had just been through several weeks of painful tests. The last one left her with a headache because of air having been left in the brain. The question *why* kept running through my mind. I had asked that question so many times and still hadn't come up with the answer I wanted to hear.

Dawn was falling asleep then—not to awake for hours. Dave and I sat there quietly, not really knowing how to give each other comfort. I think we were both so full of fear that we could not talk about it. Here they came to get our little girl. The patient escort told us we could follow them downstairs for Dawn's first stop.

Dr. Gracias, Dawn's neurosurgeon, had told us the day before that Dawn would be getting a heart catheterization. This was to be done because of the air remaining in her brain from the air test done a few days earlier. Dr. Gracias had explained that he didn't want to take a chance of air getting to Dawn's heart during surgery without his knowledge. By doing the catheterization, he could monitor her heart during surgery.

While we were in the appropriate room awaiting Dawn's surgery, our pastor, Reverend Bud, came in He said, "Good morning, how are you?" Reverend Bud was the beloved pastor of the Wayland United Methodist Church. He is tall, dark hair and wears glasses. When he walks into a room he does so with such a caring look of concern and is always inspirational. It was not a surprise to see him there so early because he was always present when the church family needed him.

"Do you really want to know the truth?" I replied. He smiled a soft, gentle smile and gave me an understanding hug. What I really wanted to say to him was that I didn't understand why God was doing this to our little girl. But how could I make a minister understand my resentment toward God?

Reverend Bud handed me a cross on a chain that he had made from horseshoe nails, and said, "I brought this for Dawn."

"Oh, thank you. Dawn will really like this," I said. "I'll hold on to it until she is awake enough to see it."

Dawn was now coming out, ready to go upstairs for the surgery. Oh, what a long day this was to be! It was only 7:50 a.m. and already it seemed I'd been there for hours. We went with Reverend Bud to the family waiting room on the second floor. There weren't many people there our name and checked it with her list on the surgical schedule. She said, "There is coffee yet, but through the course of the day the room would be filled. The volunteer at the desk took and tea over there. Just help yourself. I will let you know when there is some news." We got some coffee and went to find a comfortable place to sit, a spot somewhat out of the way.

At first, we all made small talk, trying to get our minds off Dawn's surgery. The first procedure wasn't even the actual surgery. Dr. Gracias would have to do a surgical test—going through the top of Dawn's skull to put dye into the brain and take X-rays. What he had really been trying to tell us for days was that Dawn had a brain tumor that would be hard to find. Dr. Gracias wanted Dawn to have a cat scan because he was sure that Dawn had a brain tumor. He could not get her scheduled for a cat scan soon enough and in his oppion time was inportant and did not want to waste it with her being on a waiting list. There was only two cat scaners in the State of Michigan and both were booked up for another week. He explained that even though all the tests pointed to it, none of them proved it. He said you can't operate on the brain like you can the stomach to explore for what you're trying to find. You have to know exactly what you are going into the brain for. You then try to correct the problem and get out. There is a possibility of much nerve damage when operating on one's brain.

Dr. Gracias had given us a long list of things that could result because of his surgery. Most of them were so scary that we couldn't even grasp them. I resented his telling us about them, even though I knew it was part of his job. I tried to join in the conversation, but most of the time my mind kept wandering off to the days of the past, days when Dawn was a happy, healthy tomboy. I liked those thoughts better than the present ones, so I let my mind drift back to when my children were born.

On April 25, 1963, our beautiful daughter, Lori Ann, was born. She was perfect in every way, but because of prolonged labor, she had a hard time breathing and had to be put under"mist," which helped her breathe better.

Exactly two years later on April 25, 1965, our second daughter, Dawn Marie, was born. Her birth went very well. The labor and delivery were normal and short, compared to my first one. The only problem was that Dawn was a girl, and we both hoped for a boy. Doesn't every couple want a boy the second time around if a girl comes first? I can remember saying to Dave when I came out of delivery, "We have another daughter, just like Lori. I'm sorry I didn't give you a son." Dave reassured me that it didn't matter; there would be another time to have a son.

The years that went by while the girls were toddlers were extremely happy ones. Lori was always the one who wanted to be dressed in pretty, girlish clothes, while Dawn was the tomboy type and wanted to wear pants all the time. Lori had long, thick curls while Dawn had thin but pretty, short blonde hair. Each had her own personality. That was very obvious. Lori wanted to play with dolls and with the neighbor girls, while Dawn always played with the boys. Anytime I couldn't find Dawn, I looked down the street at Jeff Clark's house. Jeff was the same age as Dawn, and they got along well together. Those two kids were always causing his mother, Bonnie, and me to be concerned, because they had no fear of the dangers around them. They were always wandering away from their homes. It seemed like an endless battle trying to teach them the danger of crossing the street.

The time on the clock seemed like it was ticking away very slowly.

I said, "Dave, how long do you think it will be before they let us know what they found in that X-ray test?"

"I don't know, but it shouldn't be too long now."

My nerves were starting to get edgy."Oh, dear God, please let Dawn be all right. Please don't let her have anything that can't be fixed."

I got up and walked around the room. There were many people there. Some of them looked worried, like me, while others appeared to have no worry at all. *Oh, here comes Dr. Gracias. Oh, my gosh, he doesn't look too happy.* He walked into the room slowly looking down with a sad face. As Dr. Gracias approached me, Dave and Reverend Bud got up and joined us.

Dr. Gracias blurted out, "We've found the problem. Dawn does have a tumor. We've checked out the X-rays, and now we're going to go in after it." I could see by the excited look on his face that after all the tests that had been down he knew right where to go in after the tumor and did not what to wast more time in getting it out. With a smile and a few words of encouragement, he left. I started crying, and Dave took me in his arms and said, "We've got to pray and trust that Dr. Gracias will get it without damage to her brain."

"Oh Dave, that won't happen, will it?"

Reverend Bud spoke up and said, "Let's sit down and pray." We bowed our heads and said a comforting prayer, but I still felt very scared, and he could sense that.

He said, "Marilyn, you knew all along that Dawn's problem was probably a tumor, didn't you?"

Still in tears, I said, "Yes, but I was so hoping that they'd be wrong."

It took me a while to get my composure. It was now 11:30 a.m. Dr. Gracias had said it would be several hours before they could tell us anything more. Just about that time, our good friends, Karen and Bill Doubblestein, arrived. I ran to them, half-crying, trying to tell them what had happened. They suggested we go down to the coffee shop. I was too nervous to eat, but agreed to go with them. As we sipped coffee, I kept thinking, *How can anyone laugh today? My little girl is in surgery, fighting for her life.*

Dr. Gracias had said Dawn could become paralyzed because of this surgery. *Oh, dear God, you can't let that happen.* I tried to keep my mind on the conversation at the table, but I felt I was there in body only. Before Bill and Karen left, we went to the chapel and prayed.

Upon our return to the surgical waiting room, started our waiting game again.

I looked at the clock, which said 1:00 p.m. It seemed like a long time since Dr. Gracias had come out and talked to us. For the next hour, I did pretty well. I managed to talk about church affairs and even tried to smile at Dave's and Reverend Bud's small talk. As the clock ticked on, I watched the faces of the different doctors that came through the door. One came in all smiles and told members of a family that their patient was out of surgery and doing well. That doctor had a smile on his face as he came through the door, so I knew he was going to give that family good news. I watched other doctors come through who weren't smiling, and the news they told matched the looks on their faces. I found myself studying the face of every doctor who came through that door. I said, "I sure hope Dr. Gracias has a smile on his face when he comes in." I started thinking back to when Dawn was three years old, I suffered a miscarriage. Losing the baby upset me very much. I was so sure that the baby I was carrying was a boy, so went through emotional turmoil because of my loss. I felt I'd never have a son of my own. My doctor tried to convince me that I could get pregnant again and everything would probably turn out fine.

Well, the doctor was right. Thirteen months after the miscarriage, I gave birth to a beautiful son on July 27, 1969. Dave and I were very excited. When I came out of the delivery room, I cried from happiness. We named our son D.J., for Dave, Jr.. When D.J. was three, he had to have tubes put in his ears because of fluid in his inner ears. At the time, I thought it was a big deal. I had to leave him at the hospital overnight. I hated leaving my little boy in that big hospital.

———————•———•———•———————

Three years later, I was waiting in the hospital with my nine-year-old daughter lying on a surgical table. The thought of those doctors cutting into her brain scare me. *How do I keep my mind off what's going on?* The time seemed endless, even though the clock on the wall was ticking away. I was pacing the floor not being able sit. My head was aching and I had an upset stomach which causes me to make frequent trips to the bathroom. The fear of the unknown was really taking over my mind.

Reverend Bud sensed my nervousness and said, "God is in there with Dawn. He will guide Dr. Gracias."

Dave spoke up in his calm voice, saying, "We've got to have faith that our prayers will be answered. She'll be all right, honey."

I wonder why I don't feel the calmness they do. Why am I so scared? I couldn't sit still; I had to walk around. I walked over to the window and stared out at the walls of the adjoining wing. *Everything looks depressing today.*

I found myself wondering back in time remembering when we moved back to Wayland in 1970 from our home in GrandRapids. We decided we did not want to raise our kids in the city so bought the house from my parents that I grew up in. It was an old two story farm house that needed work but Dave had the ability to remodel it. That house was also next to my parents so the kids would be next to their Grandparents just as I was while growing up. Those first five years were so busy but such fun. Now I think what would life be like if our little girl ends up with cancer? I couldn't even bear to think of that word. It's so ugly and usually means death. *Please, God, please don't let that happen to our Dawn.* I glanced up at the clock. It was only 4:00p.m. *Oh please, let this ordeal be over! I can't take much more of this waiting.* It seemed like forever since they came and took Dawn from her room at 6:45 that morning. After making another trip to the bathroom, I tried to sit down and relax. My stomach felt like a ball of knots. After all, why should I believe everything was going to be all right? The doctors took weeks just trying to diagnose her problem.

Thinking back to the beginning of Dawn's problems, I felt frustrated that I didn't see the signs earlier. I could trace the trouble all the way back to the previous November. Dawn had always been our tomboy. She was always energetic and on the go. I noticed that all of a sudden she would come home from school and sit around. It was so unlike her.

I remember saying, "Dawn, what's the matter with you? Why don't you want to change your clothes and play?"

Dawn's only reply was, "I don't feel like it."

I couldn't understand it at the time, so I just shrugged it off. On Thanksgiving, Dawn lay around all day. She didn't really seem sick, but she didn't act like herself. She looked tired. I thought she might be coming down with the flu.

I discussed Dawn with my mother who said, "Marilyn, don't worry. Dawn's probably going through a growing stage."

As time went on, Dawn started to complain more. She would persistently say her stomach ached. Usually she'd complain in the morning when she'd get up early to go to school.

I finally took her to Dr. Taylor, her pediatrician. He gave her an exam and said, "I really can't find anything wrong. I think we should do stomach X-rays just to be sure." The X-rays showed nothing. I really didn't know whether I should be happy or not.

Naturally, I didn't want them to find something wrong, yet I wanted an answer to Dawn's problem.

As time went on, Dawn's complaints continued. In January, Dawn came home with her report card. I watched her get off the bus and noticed she wasn't walking very straight. When she came through the door, she handed me her report card and headed right for the couch. I was shocked to see her grades had fallen off considerably. Dawn had been an A and B student. Her grades had fallen to Cs and Ds. I asked Dawn why her grades had gone down. She said in a whiny discouraged upset voice, "I don't know. I tried." I decided to call her teacher, Mrs. Garza, and find out what she had to say. She told me Dawn had been doing very poorly. She went on to say that Dawn would often put her head on the desk. I decided that another trip to the doctor was due. I started thinking maybe Dawn had anemia. That would explain her being tired all the time.

Dr. Taylor again gave Dawn a thorough exam and a series of blood tests. I felt even more frustrated the second time.

Dr. Taylor asked, "Is Dawn having problems with the teacher or classmates at school?"

I answered, "No, she's always liked school and gotten along very well."

He went on to say, "There might be a psychological problem that you're not aware of. I suggest you check out any problem there might be at school. If she gets stomachaches only in the morning, she might be looking for a reason to stay home."

I left the doctor's office feeling really down. *Now where do I go to get my answers? Dawn likes school. She always has liked it and done very well.*

A few weeks went by, and she didn't seem to get any better. One evening I was going through some of her school papers and noticed her penmanship was really scribbly. "Oh, my gosh!" was my reaction to her work. She usually wrote so beautifully. *What is going on? Things just don't add up! There must be something wrong.*

Why can't Dr. Taylor find out what it is? The next day Dawn came in the house from school all covered with snow.

I asked, "Dawn, what happened to you?"

"I fell on my way from the bus."

This was the last straw. I had noticed that Dawn stumbled around too much lately.

In February, we made the third trip back to Dr. Taylor's office. I saw a different reaction to his exam this time. After I told him about Dawn's writing and unstable walking, he checked them out. As he watched her walk and then write, he said, "This is shocking. How long has this been going on?"

I was surprised at his remarks. I tried to explain that Dawn hadn't been herself for months and that I had brought her to his office twice before.

"I want her admitted to Butterworth Hospital tonight, so more thorough tests can be done. We have to get to the bottom of this."

I was shocked at his statements. After all, for weeks I'd been trying to convince him that something was wrong with her. A mother knows her child. A doctor doesn't see the same child that often, so he can't be expected to notice changes in his or her behavior. I felt frustrated and angry as I drove Dawn to the hospital. She had many questions that I couldn't answer.

Dawn spent a week in the hospital going through all kinds of tests. She couldn't understand what upper and lower GI tests were. Even though I tried to explain to her that the doctors were trying to find out what was wrong with her, she didn't understand. She just kept asking me when I was going to take her home. I didn't have any answers for her. I myself, had a hard time understanding all the medical talk by the doctors. An understanding intern became my link to the doctors and all their medical terminology. Anytime I went to him and asked him to explain a test that Dawn would be having, he'd explain it in detail. The only problem was that I couldn't remember what he said so as to explain it to anyone else.

I didn't realize at the time that this intern, Dr. Alcorn, would become a friend to both Dawn and me in the weeks to come.

Finally, the day came when Dr. Taylor called me into the conference room to let me know the test results. I was scared and worried about what he'd say. As Dr. Taylor and I sat down across from each other, I could feel my heart beat faster and panic sat in. I started shaking. I was very afraid of the news that was forthcoming. A lot of the tests that were done on Dawn would lead a person to think they were looking for a brain tumor. Many doctors had looked at Dawn. I'm not even sure they agreed among themselves.

As Dr. Taylor started to talk, I could feel his hesitation. He started out by saying, "Mrs. Smith, the tests that have been done on Dawn have not led us to a completely positive diagnosis. But, based upon the tests that were done and her symptoms, I feel she has chorea, also known as Saint Vitus Dance. Are you familiar with it at all?"

"No, I've never heard of it."

"It's a nervous disorder characterized by controlled jerks and twitches of the body's limbs. It can also affect speech and muscular coordination. That would explain Dawn's falling and sloppy handwriting."

I felt numb. I became overcome with shock and fear of how I would be able to handle the news. This disease sounded terrible.

"How long will she have this?"

"I'm not sure, but it will probably get worse before it gets better." He went on to say, "At least that's not as bad as a brain tumor."

I agreed and tried to act relieved. After he told me a little more about this chorea, he said that a neurologist named Dr. Van Nuis wasn't in total agreement with the diagnosis.

"Dr. Van Nuis would like you to bring Dawn to his office in a week so he can check her out again for any new signs."

I wasn't really sure what Dr. Taylor was trying to say, but I didn't like it. I felt so angry at God and nervous inside. How was I going to explain all this to Dawn and Dave.

I had mixed feelings the day I brought Dawn home from the hospital. I wanted to believe what Dr. Taylor said about her having chorea, but the idea of another doctor doubting the diagnosis bothered me. Dawn was happy to be home. I overheard her say to her cousin, "I'm not ever going back to that hospital. If they take me back, I'll jump out a window." I was shocked by her statement, but I fully understood why she'd say something like that. She had been through so many tests that week. I started thinking, *What will I do with her if she should have to go back?*

Dr. Van Nuis told me about symptoms to look for during the week that we had Dawn home. One of those symptoms was double vision. One night after supper, Dawn had gotten up from the table first and started into the living room. We heard her hit the wall. Dave and I turned around and looked. I yelled, "Dawn, what did you walk into the wall for?"

"I saw two walls," was her response.

Dave and I looked at each other and were both thinking of how this could mean trouble.

Dave responded to Dawn by saying, "How long have you been seeing two things?"

"I don't know, quite a while, I guess."

I sat there in shock. *Oh, my gosh, what does this mean?*

We had no question now that Dawn would have to go back and see Dr. Van Nuis. We did that on a Friday, and then on Sunday we took her back to the hospital. It all seemed to happen so fast that we didn't have time to think about it. Dr. Van Nuis told us at his office, "Dawn's double vision means that we have to look further into the idea that there may be a brain tumor." Oh, there was that ugly word *tumor* again.

I hated our drive back to the hospital, but it gave me the chance to talk to Dawn about her feelings. She made it very clear that she didn't like going back. She said, "Mom, am I going to be there long?" I tried to reassure her that it would only be a few days. I guess I told her that because I really wanted to believe it myself.

When we got to the hospital, Dr. Alcorn gave Dawn her admitting exam and took her history. I was so bitter about bringing her back that I wanted to tell him to go look up her records and quit asking the same questions over again. I was so bitter about the situation in general because she had been there so many times that I expected them to have good records and know more what was wrong with her. Dr. Alcorn really tried to be nice and reassured us that he would help in any way that he could. He said, "Anytime you have questions or don't understand the tests that Dawn will be going through, I'll be glad to help you."

I thanked him very politely and said, "Can you tell me why the doctors can't find Dawn's problem?"

"No, I'm sure this is very frustrating for you, but some problems are hard to find."

"In the meantime, my daughter has to go through these repeated tests while the doctors are trying to decide who's right about the diagnosis."

As the days went by and the tests Dawn went through seemed to be repeats of the ones she had previously, I became even more bitter. I tried praying, but it didn't seem to help. I tried talking to Reverend Bud, but that didn't help either. I found that Dave and I couldn't even talk together about it. We were so unhappy to see our daughter go through these tests that we took it out on each other.

I had been working part-time as a waitress in Wayland for the past two years, and when Dawn had been in the hospital the first time, I took off and spent most of my time with her. That time it was different. I found myself wanting to spend less time there. I used the excuse that I couldn't take off from work, even though I could have. The real problem was I didn't like what was going on at the hospital, so I turned my back and pretended it wasn't really happening. When arriving at the hospital I found Dawn sitting at a table in the playroom crying. I sat down by her and said, "Dawn, what's the matter?"

She said, "I had to drink that awful chalky stuff today. I had to go to the bathroom, and they told me I had to wait while they took pictures."

I took her in my arms and let her cry. My heart sank. *What have I done? I should have been here with her today. I've got to quit running from this problem and help her face it.* I knew from what she described that she had had upper and lower GI tests again today. I knew she had been through it before and figured it wouldn't bother her. I realized that any test from then on was going to have an emotional effect on her. That incident helped me make the decision to take off from work and stay with her until it was over.

While I was sitting there with Dawn, Dr. Van Nuis came by and said he wanted to talk to Dave and me. I could tell he was upset about something. He had a frown on his face as he slowly walked towards us. Later on, when Dave got to the hospital, we went to the conference room with Dr. Van Nuis. He explained to us that the tests done thus far did not yet give enough evidence to make a diagnosis. I couldn't believe what I was hearing. I said, "What does this mean?"

He went on to say that he consulted with a neurosurgeon named Dr. Gracias. "We went over all Dawn's tests, especially the EEG. Both of us feel that we should do a pneumoencephalogran test on her." He explained that air would be put up into Dawn's brain through the spine. That would allow the doctors to get better X-rays of the brain. I didn't hear anything beyond that. The test sounded so scary. *How could they do this to Dawn? How could Dave and I allow this?* I tried to get my mind back on what was being said, but I was too full of fear. We had to sign papers for the test to be done on Dawn, because it could be dangerous. Blood vessels could be misplaced, and Dr. Gracias would have to be there in case this should happen.

Dawn's test was scheduled for 11:00 a.m. on Friday, March 7th. I spent the night before and all morning with my stomach tied up in knots. Dawn asked me many questions. She especially wanted to know, "When am I going home?"

I wanted so badly to give her an encouraging answer. I was running out of ways to comfort her. Before the nurse came to give Dawn a shot—to put her to sleep—I said to her, "The test the doctors do today will help them decide what's wrong with you."

"Yes, but I don't want them to hurt me anymore."

I took her in my arms and said, "Oh Dawn, you've been so brave. I pray this is the last test you have to go through."

After the patient escort came and took Dawn, I walked over to the chairs in the lobby of the pediatric floor—I'd sat there many times. Watching the movement of the nurses and patients on the floor, I couldn't help but wonder about all the children here on the floor and all the different ailments they had. I was envious of the parents who had children here for routine problems, like having their tonsils out. As I looked up, Reverend Bud walked onto the floor from the elevator. I was glad to see him. I think he sensed right away that I was scared to death. The first thing he said was, "How are you?"

Almost in tears, I admitted, "I'm extremely afraid something is going to happen to Dawn today." He asked me why I was so afraid. I told him how I had overheard someone say that our children belong to God, and sometimes He chooses to take them back. "I'm scared I've done something wrong and that God is going to take Dawn away from me."

Reverend Bud put his hand on mine and said, "God does not punish us through our children."

I really needed to hear him say that, because I was convinced that I was being punished.

By the time Dave came from work, I was calm, but not relaxed. The three of us sat and tried to talk about positive things. After a couple of hours, I saw Dr. Van Nuis and Dr. Gracias coming down the hallway and I knew the test was over. The look on their faces told me something was wrong. Panic came over me as we met them in the lobby.

"What's wrong?" I yelled out to them. I could feel my heart beating faster.

Dr. Van Nuis said, "We'd like to talk to you in the conference room."

I could feel the fear taking over. I didn't want to go in. I didn't want to hear what they had to say.

Dr. Van Nuis started by telling us, "Dawn is okay. The test went smoothly. She'll sleep for the rest of the day. We don't want her to wake up because when she does she'll have a terrible headache. We'll have to keep her head flat for three days until the air releases from her brain."

Oh, how awful this sounds. What have they done to my little girl? How am I going to explain this to her?

Dr. Gracias took over and said, "The test showed there is something wrong, but we can't be sure what it is or where." He went on to explain all the medical terminology, but I turned myself off. I didn't want to hear anymore. I was having a hard time fighting back the tears. What I did hear him say was, "We want to send Dawn to Detroit for a CAT scan." He explained, "CAT scan is a sophisticated X-ray machine that takes more detailed pictures of the brain than a conventional one. There are only two here in Michigan—one in Detroit and one in Ann Arbor. There will be no pain for Dawn other than the needle used to shoot dye in her veins."

All I could think about while Dr. Gracias was talking was how I told Dawn this morning that the test they did that day would probably be the last one. Then they told me they'd have to send her to a strange hospital for another one. *Oh, dear God, when is this all going to end?*

Dave and I left the hospital that night without even seeing Dawn. I was glad she was sleeping so well, that way I didn't have to face her with the news. The ride home was quiet. Neither of us wanted to talk about the problems the doctors were trying so desperately to solve. There was not much doubt left; they were looking for a brain tumor.

The next day, Dave and I went to the hospital together. I was relieved to find Dawn still sleeping when we arrived. We quietly pulled up chairs and sat by her bed in silence. Dr. Alcorn walked into the room, and by the look on his face. He walked slowly with his head down and a frown. He wasn't bearing good news. He asked us how we were and said, "Dawn slept through the night". Dr. Gracias will be along soon, because he wants to talk to you." *Oh no,* I thought, *what now?*

Dr. Gracias again took us into the conference room. I didn't like the look on his face. I was beginning to be obsessed with trying to read the expressions on doctors' faces, and his expression and a frown on his face looked like bad news. Dr. Gracias said to us, "Dawn *can't* be taken to Detroit. They are too busy over there and can't schedule a CAT scan for two weeks. I don't feel we have that much time. If there is a tumor, I don't feel we can wait two weeks to find it. I want to do a surgical test on Dawn that will pinpoint the problem so if there is a tumor, I know where to find it. A doctor can't operate on the brain like one does the stomach. You can't explore and look for the problem by doing surgery. When you operate on the brain, you have to know exactly what you are after."

By the time he got done explaining everything, I was much confused. Dave and I didn't know a thing about this doctor, yet he wanted us to give him permission to cut into our daughter's brain. That sounded so terrible and scary, I could feel myself getting so worked up that I hardly heard what he said. The word *tumor* kept ringing in my ear, and I didn't like it.

By the time we left the hospital that evening, all the doctors who had been on Dawn's case convinced us that the surgical test should be done. The hospital staff, we knew, spoke very highly of Dr. Gracias and said Dawn would be in the best of hands. Dave and I were both impressed with him when he said, "I have children of my own, and two of them are twin boys about the same age as Dawn." I felt he at least knew what it was like to be a parent. He also said, "I will take every precaution. Kids are very special to me. On the way home, I suggested to Dave that we stop by and see our friends Karen and Bill. I needed to talk to Karen for she is a nurse and would talk straight with me. Being of strong faith I wanted them to pray with us." I had a hard time with the idea of Dawn's brain being cut into.

Karen and Bill welcomed us with a warm embrace and listened to all our fears. Karen was able to see things from a medical standpoint and gently said to me, "Marilyn, Dr. Gracias is a neurosurgeon. He knows his field of surgery as well as a doctor that operates on your stomach for gallbladder. He regularly does surgery on the brain. Before Dave and I left the four of us sat in a circle and prayed that God would be with Dr. Gracias during surgery which gave me a sense of peace.

I didn't sleep well that night, because I kept hearing Dr. Gracias say, "I have to cut into the top of Dawn's brain, put dye in, and get a different set of X-rays." The words that haunted me were *cut into.* Those two words kept going through my mind until I felt like I wanted to explode. Finally I started crying, held in Dave's arms, until I had no energy left. That was the first night since Dawn entered the hospital that Dave and I talked and took comfort from each other.

———————◆———————

We sat in the family waiting room, waiting for the results of the surgery. Just a few days before I was afraid for Dr. Gracias to cut into Dawn's head. Now I waited while he tried to remove a tumor. *Oh, Lord, please don't let this tumor be cancerous.*

I heard Reverend Bud's voice saying, "Marilyn, where are your thoughts? You don't seem to be here in this room."

"I've been thinking over the last few weeks, when Dawn went through all her tests. Much has happened in a short time."

I again glanced at the clock. It was after 5:00 p.m. The room had emptied. The only people left besides Reverend Bud, Dave, and me was a family over in the corner. They didn't appear to be anxious about their patient. As I continued looking around the room, I seen the empty chairs from what had been a busy day. Even the volunteer lady had left. The door opened and a doctor walked in with a smile on his face. He went to the family in the corner. I could tell from their smiles that they received good news. My thoughts were dear God, please let Dr. Gracias come smiling through the door like that, with good news.

As time went on, I got more up tight and wondered what was taking so long. The door opened again, and this time Reverend Bill walked in. I ran to him and expressed my fears.

He gave me a warm embrace and said, "Just remember, Marilyn, God is there with Dawn. She's not alone." We then sat down and talked about the events of the day.

As we talked, my mother, my sister Willie, and her husband Louie arrived. I was surprised but happy to see them. My mother gave me a warm hug and said, "We were concerned when we didn't hear from you, so we decided to come and find out how things were going. I filled them in on what we knew, which wasn't much.

The phone rang, and Reverend Bud answered it. A nurse from surgery called to say that the major part of the surgery was over and that Dr. Gracias was putting in a shunt. I asked Reverend Bud what the nurse meant by that. He said, "The nurse said Dr. Gracias will explain everything to us when he finishes. It will be another hour or so." I couldn't understand why this was taking so long. It had to be bad news.

It seemed like the time was just dragging by now. Everyone sat in silence most of the time. The time on the clock was 7:30

p.m.. Just then the door opened, and Dr. Gracias walked through, still in his surgical clothes. *Oh no, I don't like the look on his face. His head was down and he had the sadest look of bewilderment. It's not the happy one I've been waiting for.* I walk toward him, almost afraid to hear what he had to say.

Dealing with Depression

Dr. Gracias said, "Please, let's all sit down." My heart sank right there, and I panicked. I felt sure that he was going to give us bad news. All of a sudden, there was a dreaded silence in the room. I could feel Dr. Gracias's sadness as he tried to speak. He started by saying, "I'm sorry, folks, but Dawn's tumor was cancerous. I removed as much as I could, but I didn't get it all. If I'd taken any more, I would have destroyed her eyesight."

The room was no longer silent. It exploded with hysterics from Dave and me. I couldn't believe what I was hearing. I cried uncontroably with my hands on face stuping over with head in lap. Dave paced the floor crying making a fist wanting to bust up the furniture.

With tears running down my face and Reverend Bud trying to comfort me, I said to Dr. Gracias, "What does this mean?"

Dr. Gracias said, "We'll have to treat the rest of Dawn's tumor with radiation." He tried to explain the surgery and the results, but I couldn't hear anything beyond the fact that the tumor was cancerous. I just kept saying to myself this is just a bad dream blocking out the pain of what he was saying. I did hear Dave say, "Will Dawn die?"

Dr. Gracias very slowly said, "If the radiation has a positive effect on the tumor, she might live three to five years."

I asked, "If it doesn't?"

"It might be only six months," he said.

I was hysterical. I could hear Dave yelling, but I didn't understand what he was saying. I'd never seen Dave break down and cry like that. It was so unlike him. He later relayed to me that, at that moment, he was in a rage. He was so frustrated that he walked around the room wanting to bust up a chair to release his tension.

After all of us spent time crying in anguish at what we heard, we spent twenty minutes crying on each others shoulder sometimes sitting sometimes standing. Bill said, "Dr. Gracias, would you like to pray with us?" After his affirmative reply, we formed a circle, and Bill prayed. I was so overwhelmed with my grief that I didn't hear a word he said. Afterward, Dr. Gracias offered a sedative to me help me cope.

I snapped back and said, "Will that change anything or give my little girl back her good health?"

He then said in a very stern upset tone, "Dawn is up there fighting for her life. She *is* already starting to wake up. She needs you now more than ever." Trying to fight his emotions, he said to us, "Dawn will be going to her room soon. I expect you to be there when she wakes up." He then departed very quickly. I knew he was having as hard a time as we all were. The only difference was he couldn't let his emotions show.

Just as Dr. Gracias closed the door, I yelled out, "I want to be there for Dawn!" But it was too late; he didn't hear me. As my family tried to comfort us, they suggested that I take Dr. Gracias's advice and take the sedative. I don't like drugs but finally agreed I should to calm me down.

As we continued to grieve, the news came that Dawn was in her room. I told the people in the room, "Okay, I'll take the shot so I can go see Dawn." A nurse was there almost instantly with the shot. As she gave it to me, I said, "I wish this shot could change this nightmare for us." She didn't know how to answer me. She looked at me as if to say I'm sorry and then left.

We waited a short time until we got our emotions under control and then went upstairs. Dawn had been put in the intensive care unit on the pediatric floor. The ICU was crowded with several beds, which were mostly cribs with babies. The nurses' desk was in the middle. As we entered the room, I spotted Dawn close to the door. The sight of her startled me so much that I ran out of the room crying. I put my arms around my sister Willie and said, "Dawn looks terrible. She has tubes in her, and there is yellow stuff all over her chest." Willie tried to calm me down, but I kept crying, thinking of the scene I just saw. I kept saying, "This can't be happening."

Dr. Gracias walked by and went into the room. I heard him call Dawn's name, so I had to straighten myself out and get in there. I wiped my eyes and walked back into the room. Dr. Gracias was standing over Dawn checking her condition. He said, "Dawn, move your feet." She responded by moving her feet. He said, "Dawn, move your arms." Again she responded by moving her arms. She was trying to wake up. She opened her eyes part way and started crying. Dr. Gracias kept checking Dawn's eyes and when he was through, he said, "Dawn is doing real well. The tests I just did with her show me that there is no brain damage from the surgery."

I was still having a hard time with the way she looked. Her head was all bandaged; there was yellow iodine all down her chest; a heart monitor was hooked up, and she had a catheter going into her bladder. I could see several bandages from her neck to her abdomen. I asked Dr. Gracias about them, and he said, "There are incisions made on Dawn's neck and down her chest because of the shunt we put in." He went on to explain that the shunt was put in from Dawn's brain down to her abdomen to drain off fluid. The tumor was causing extra fluid on the brain that couldn't escape through the ventricles. A valve in Dawn's brain(that could be felt under the skin on her head) would pump the extra fluid from the brain down thin tubing that goes from the head to the abdomen and empties out. Everything he tried to explain to us was all new, and I was too tired and upset to really understand it all. As I looked at Dawn, I tried to reach out with arms and hold her, but the fear of what she was thinking kept me at a distance. The thought that crept into my mind was Dawn's acceptance of all this and if whe would blame me for her condition. I had told her we were at the end. Now I find out this surgery is only another chapter. Dawn lay very still opening her eyes just a little with a sad look of fear.

As Dawn fell off to sleep, the nurse walked over and said, "You folks should go home and get some sleep."

I snapped back, "No, I can't leave her."

Dr. Gracias spoke up and said, "You really should go home. It's been a long day for you." After the nurse and Dr. Gracias finished talking to us about how the nurses would be with Dawn and they'd call if anything developed, we decided to leave. The head nurse on the 11:00 p.m. to 7:00 a.m. shift was Jan. She was from Wayland. After coming on duty, she reassured us that Dawn was special, and she'd take good care of her. She gave me a warm embrace and said, "You look like you could use some sleep."

I admitted she was right by saying, "Okay, I'll go home if you promise to call me if Dawn wakes up and wants me." She said she would. We knew that Dr. Gracias had already left but not without leaving a lot of instructions. I hated to leave, but I was too exhausted to argue, and Jan seemed to be sincere about her concern.

When we got back to the lobby, I was surprised to see that Reverend Bud was still here. It was 1:30 a.m., and he'd been here all day with us. I said to him, "You're still *here?*"

He answered, "I wanted to make sure you were both okay before I left."

I said, "Thank you for being with us today. I still can't believe this has all happened."

As Dave and I drove home, I kept going over the day's events in my mind. I kept wondering how I would explain the news to Lori and D.J.

How can they understand the meaning of all this? Lori is eleven years old, and D.J. is only five. How do I tell a five-year-old that his sister has cancer and might die?

Dave and I spent a restless night. I kept hoping I'd go to sleep and wake up to find that this was all a nightmare. Morning came and the phone hadn't rung during the few hours that had passed. I called the hospital at 6:00 a.m., and they said, "Dawn slept all night." That was some comfort. I didn't want her to know I had left her.

As I prepared to go to the hospital that morning, I kept wondering how I would tell Lori and D.J. about their sister. There didn't seem to be a right way to discuss a small child having cancer. Dave went to work, so I didn't have him there to help me. I somehow had to find a way to talk about something I didn't understand or want to believe.

When Lori and D.J. got ready for school, I explained that I would be going to the hospital every day for a while. As I went on about Dawn's surgery and the recovery time she'd need, I realized that my family had already talked to them. D.J. said, "Mom, will you be here when I get home from school?" That question made me realize a five-year-old was too young to understand all the problems that would occur now. *How am I going to divide my time between the hospital that has my sick daughter and the home where I am also needed?* I kissed the kids as they went to the bus and said, "Go to Grandma's after school. I'll see you later tonight." As I watched them walk to the bus, I couldn't stop my tears of despair and thoughts of how I was going to handle this.

My first day of sitting with Dawn in ICU was very trying. She slept most of the time, but when she was awake she cried. I couldn't get her to respond to me. A student nurse, Beth, was assigned to sit right by her and keep track of her vital signs every hour.

Beth gave me a pretty pink scarf for Dawn. She said, "Dawn will want something on her head when she gets the bandage off."

I thanked her and said, "I haven't thought ahead to the fact that Dawn's head will be bare." I reached over and put the scarf in Dawn's nightstand and found a small brown bag. As I opened the bag, Beth noticed the shocked look on my face. Without saying anything, I showed her Dawn's blonde hair inside.

"Oh, I'm so sorry you found Dawn's hair that way."

"Why did they put Dawn's hair in this bag?"

"They have to. The hospital hangs on to anything that belongs to a patient, so Dawn's hair has to be disposed of by you."

I could understand the policy, but I expressed my feeling of resentment at seeing my daughter's hair in a brown bag. I told the nurse she should have given it to me with a warning of what it was and then I put it in the wastebasket.

During the next few days, going to the hospital was a real chore. I would walk into ICU each morning, hoping to find a change in Dawn. She was showing signs of severe depression, and I didn't know how to handle it. It's been four days since surgery and Dawn still was not taking. I never thought the surgery would have such a empact on her. I kept talking to her but all I got back was blank looks. I spent the days with her, and Dave joined me after work in the evenings. While she was in ICU, the only other visitors that she was allowed to have were Reverend Bud and my parents.

Dr. Gracias said Dawn's recovery was coming along well, but she still did not respond to me. She just sat and stared right through me. She was not eating enough food, either. I keep telling her, Dr Gracias said Dawn's recovery was coming along well but she was still not responding to me. She would stare at me with such sadness on her face not touching her food while I kept saying, "Dawn, if you don't eat, you won't get better." She just looked at me as if to say, "I don't believe you anymore." I wanted to pick her up out of bed and tell the doctors to leave her alone. I felt sorry for her, but knew I could not let it show for it would only hinder her recovery.

On Sunday, Dave and I went to the hospital together. We went with the idea that *today* we were going to get Dawn to eat and start fighting to recover. When we walked into ICU, we found her just lying in bed with her dinner in front of her. I said, "Dawn, why aren't you eating?"

At first she just looked at us, but finally she said, "I don't like it."

I was so surprised. She hadn't said anything to us since she had surgery on Tuesday. Dave kept talking to her until he got her to eat a little bit. The nurse that was taking care of her today said, "Dawn has been sitting all morning. I had a hard time giving her a bath."

Dr. Gracias was off this weekend, so his partner, Dr. Hill, came to see Dawn. He checked her all over and then said, "Has Dawn been out of bed yet?" After my negative reply, he asked, "How long has it been since she had surgery?"

"Five days," I answered.

He gave a disgusted look as to be saying why has this child not been out of bed when he checked her chart and said, "Dawn should be up and going to the bathroom. She has to start moving around on her own." Dr. Hill left some new instructions with the nurse, one of which was to have Dawn start walking.

As soon as the doctor left, the nurse said to me, "Would you help me get Dawn up?" I agreed, so we proceeded to try to walk her to the bathroom. After the first couple steps, Dawn screamed, "No! No!" Her legs were just like spaghetti. We did all we could do to keep her from falling. She screamed all the way to the bathroom and back. She made me feel like I was really hurting her.

Dawn was quiet the rest of the day. Dave and I took turns going to the lobby to mingle with the number of visitors who kept coming to see us. I was so upset about Dawn's reaction to getting out of bed that I had a hard time leaving her for very long. Everyone who came to see us remarked about how tired I looked. I was tired, but I was also hurting inside. Dealing with Dawn's depression was taking its toll on me.

When we got to my mother's that night to pick up the kids, we found D.J. sitting at the table having a snack. When he heard Mother and me discussing Dawn, he spoke up and said, "Mom, I'm sick. You have to stay home with me tomorrow." I felt his head; he didn't appear to have a fever.

I looked at my mother and said, "I think he wants my attention."

She said, "Yes, Marilyn, he really misses you."

Now I really feel frustrated. Dawn needs me, and my kids at home need me, too. How do I divide up my time? Dave spoke up and said, "You should stay home with D.J. tomorrow and let your mother sit with Dawn."

I told him I couldn't go all day without seeing her. My Mother had offered to go but after much discussion, we decided that I'd go to the hospital in the mornings. I'd leave early in order to spend time with Lori and D.J.

The next Wednesday was a happy day. Dr. Gracias came in Dawn's room in the morning, checked her over, and said, "Dawn, how would you like to get out of here today?" She nodded her head yes. He looked at me and said, "Mom, we're going to move Dawn out of ICU and into a ward with some other girls. She has been in here nine days. I feel that she's doing well enough and that she'll make better progress in a room where she can have a TV and visitors." I agreed with him completely and was delighted to have her moved where she could have a TV.

The move down the hall to a four-bed girls' ward seemed to help ease Dawn's depression. She responded to me a little better, and when visitors came to see her, she'd perk up a little.

Family, relatives, and friends started making visits the next few days. The cards Dawn received were filling her wall. Many people that we hadn't heard from in a long time were sending notes of prayers and good cheer.

Just about the time I thought things were getting better, I found Dawn going backward again. She had been in her new room for ten days. She got upset because her roommates were changing almost daily. The room had four beds, and Dawn was the only girl who was there beyond a few days. She kept saying she wanted to go home, yet she was eating less. She started giving the nurses a hard time when they'd try to care for her needs. She had lots of blood tests, and every time they came to take blood, she'd scream and cry. Dawn's veins were small, so blood was hard to get from her.

Everyone who came to her room would try to cheer her up. Dr. Alcorn would stop every time he was on the floor. He'd talk to Dawn and then ask me if I had any questions. I found him so easy to talk to and explain my feelings to. Reverend Bud came by almost daily and used his humor on Dawn. Nevertheless, her mood continued to worsen. One day I said, "Reverend Bud, I just don't know what to do anymore. Dawn's depression is getting worse."

He said, "She wants to go home. We have to make her believe that it will happen as soon as she is strong enough."

"But I've been trying," I said. "I've asked her if she has any questions, and she just won't talk to me. I get so discouraged."

Very gently he said, "You have to let God help her."

One of the girls in Dawn's room, Amy, had been there a few days. I'd talked to her mother, Diane, several times.

That night Dawn was very cross during supper. She didn't like anything on her tray, and I couldn't convince her to eat. The nurse even sent down for a chocolate shake, Dawn's favorite, to see if she'd drink that. She just kept pushing things away while staring at me. The look on her face was very depressing. It showed such sadness, eyes down as if to show me how mad she was.

Diane and Amy were watching but trying not to be obvious about it. I felt ashamed of Dawn's behavior but had much sympathy for her. I found myself saying to Diane, "Dawn is tired of the food. She's been here so long."

Diane commented, "Dawn probably misses your home cooking." Those few words that passed between us started a conversation and friendship.

The next day, with Dawn still being uncooperative and depressed, I broke down and cried. Dawn had gotten to the point where she had shut everyone out. She wouldn't even cooperate with Dr. Alcorn, and he had been her favorite. I found myself discussing my feelings with Diane, because she appeared to be a strong Christian woman.

I told Diane some of Dawn's history. She shared my feelings about why Dawn was so depressed. She said, "Marilyn, you have to let go of Dawn and turn her over to God. You're trying to be more than a mother. You have to let God handle her." I wasn't sure I understood her, but the longer we talked, the more what she said made sense.

When I went to bed that night, I prayed about Dawn's depression with a different approach. I said, "God, I can't handle Dawn's problems anymore. I'm turning her over to you. If you want Dawn to live, please help her. I want your will to be done, and not mine." I talked to God so long that I ended up falling asleep. When I woke up the next morning, I had a whole different outlook. I felt a large burden had been lifted from my shoulders. I felt relaxed with no headache or muscle tension.

When I got to the hospital that morning, I found Dawn sitting in a chair eating her breakfast. I was very pleasantly surprised. I approached her and said, "Dawn, how do you feel today?"

"Better," she said.

"Wonderful!" I said, as I bent down and kissed her. The whole day went so well that I couldn't wait for Diane to come and visit Amy so I could tell her about it.

This experience seemed to be a turning point in Dawn's recovery and in my spiritual life. I went home that night and thanked God for His love. I began, the next morning and every morning after that, to read His Scriptures; then I closed each time with a prayer for strength.

Dr. Gracias had become so concerned about Dawn's depression that he asked a clinical psychologist to talk with her. After the psychologist talked to Dawn, he questioned me. He seemed to be concerned about whether or not I could handle Dawn after I got her home. I convinced him that Dawn's depression was due to all she had been through. "She needs to go home," I said. After talking to me for some time, he wrote on Dawn's chart that she should be discharged as soon as possible.

During the next couple days, the doctors spent time with me, preparing me for Dawn's homecoming. Dr. Gillis, the radiologist, came and talked to me about her radiation treatments. The first thing he said was, "The name of Dawn's tumor is cerebellar medulloblastoma, which is quite common in children." The long name scared me until he went on to say, "This tumor is receptive to radiation, so there is a good chance we can put it in remission."

I could have hugged this man I had just met. I said to him, "Thank you for this bit of hope that you have given me. I have been very discouraged since Dawn's surgery."

He gave me a warm smile and said, "I'll do everything I can for Dawn with radiation. There is a good chance we can beat this thing." He explained Dawn had to go back to the hospital five days a week for five weeks of radiation treatments. His medical terminology was more than my simple mind could absorb.

Finally, the big day came for Dawn to go home. My mother rode to the hospital with me.

As we walked into the hospital, I said, "Well, this is the last time we have to come visit Dawn."

When we walked into Dawn's room, I expected to find her sitting up in bed, eagerly waiting for me, but instead she was sleeping. I walked over and touched her face. She felt so warm that panic struck me as I said, "Dawn, wake up. You're going home today." She looked up at me, but there was no excitement on her face. "Dawn," I said, "what's the matter? Don't you feel well?"

"No," she said in a whiny voice.

I quickly called for a nurse who came and took Dawn's temperature. I said, "Does she have a fever?"

Dawn's nurse that day was Beverly—one of my favorites. She looked at me with a long face and said, "I'm sorry, but her temperature is 103°."

"Why?" I said, almost in tears. "What seems to be wrong?"

Beverly didn't know, but she said, "I'll call Dr. Alcorn right now."

I reached out to my mother and said, "Oh, Mom, I bet we won't take Dawn home today."

As we sat by Dawn, waiting for Dr. Alcorn, we visited with the other parents in the room. One mother said she had been there since breakfast and Dawn hadn't touched her food at all. She said, "I wondered then if there was something wrong with her."

Dr. Alcorn came in with his usually bubbly personality and said, "What's wrong with my favorite girl?" Dawn looked at him but never said a word. He checked her all over and then said, "Her right ear is inflamed. She has an ear infection."

I was shocked. "How could this happen?" I asked.

He explained that it was not uncommon for someone with low resistance to get a common infection. "We'll put Dawn on an antibiotic right away."

"When will she be able to go home?" I questioned.

"We'll keep her a couple more days and see how it goes."

I asked Dr. Alcorn to explain this latest setback to her. I didn't have the heart to let her down.

Dr. Alcorn did a terrific job of explaining to Dawn about her ear infection. She was disappointed, but she didn't get all upset like I feared she would.

As the day went on and the news traveled about Dawn's staying, many nurses and doctors stopped by to cheer her up.

One nurse, Jan, who had taken care of her right from the start, said to Dawn, "We like you so much we hate to give you up."

Dawn just frowned and said, "I'm not staying much longer." The idea that the nurses liked her well enough to keep her didn't make much of an impression.

I think the next couple days were as hard on me as they were on Dawn. I was so eager to have her home that I had to force myself to go to the hospital. Lori and D. J. were excited about Easter coming and kept talking about that. I kept telling them that Easter wouldn't be happy unless Dawn was home and we were all together. The next couple days were hard on both Dave& I.We wanted Dawn to be home for Easter. Lori and DJ were so excited about Easter and our minds were on Dawn.

On March 29th, Dawn seemed to be improved, and her fever was down. Dr. Alcorn came in and said, "Dawn, you are doing much better. How would you like to go home tomorrow?" She got so excited that I thought she would hop out of bed. Dr. Alcorn went on to say that he had talked to Dr. Taylor that morning, and he had said Dawn was improved enough to go home, although she'd have to stay on her medication for another week.

I was happy about taking her home but wondered if I should've gotten my hopes up again. There had been so many disappointments the last few weeks that I became a pessimist. My mind wandered back to what had happened during that time.

I was thankful to belong to a caring church and family. It would have been much harder dealing with all that alone. Leaving Lori and D.J. so much had my heart torn between hospital and home. I thought about the time Lori got sick with a strep infection. My mother took her to the doctor and stayed at our home with her. I should have been the one that took her but I was too wrapped up in Dawn's depression. Lori's infection cleared up in a few days, and I was wishing Dawn could get well that easily.

When Dave came to the hospital that night, Dawn and I were waiting to tell him the good news. He kidded around with her and had her laughing. It was good to see her laugh again. The parents and girls who shared Dawn's room were all excited, too. They said they would pray for her to go home.

The night seemed to go by slowly. We watched TV with Dawn and listened to all the movement around the ward. The other girls in the room had quite a few visitors. I kept thinking about the many friends and relatives who had been up several times to see Dawn. The wall in front of her bed was filled with cards and get-well wishes. Her bed was full of stuffed animals and the night stand with coloring books, funny books, and nightgowns. There were also several plants and vases of flowers about her area of the room. I decided maybe I should start packing up some of these things. I spoke to Dawn about it, and she nodded her head in agreement.

Just as I was taking down the cards, Dr. Gillis entered the room. He said, "We're going to take Dawn down for her first radiation treatment in the morning."

I said to him, with concern, "Will she still be able to go home?"

Smiling, he said, "Oh my yes." I know all about Dawn's going home. We'll have her down and back in time for her to go. We know how eager she is." Dr. Gillis then went over to Dawn and said right to her, "I wouldn't let anything get in the way of your going home. Your treatment won't take long."

As she looked at him, she said, "Will it hurt?"

He took her hand, squeezed it, and said, "You won't feel a thing."

After Dr. Gillis left, Dawn seemed very quiet and depressed. I knew she was thinking about the radiation treatments, but I didn't want to say anything more about them. I felt Dr. Gillis had said enough. In the back of my mind, I really wanted to forget that she even had to undergo the treatment.

The next morning we were all excited about Dawn's homecoming. Lori and D. J. went off to school happy, too. They were both so glad that we would be home at night now instead of running up to the hospital. When D.J. said good-bye, he also said, "I'll see you tonight, huh, Ma?"

I kissed him and said, "Yes, son, we'll all be home together tonight."

So many times the last few weeks I'd seen the anxious look in that little guy's face. He had been too young to understand the seriousness of Dawn's illness. How could he understand why we had been with her all the time and not with him?

Soon after Dave and I arrived at the hospital the next morning, we took Dawn down to the radiology unit. A couple of guys in white jackets met us and explained the procedure. Dawn was taken, first, into a room where Dr. Gillis put red marks on her head and neck. He explained that the radiotherapy field would be on the brain and spine. As he explained more, he said, "There could be quite a bit of damage because of the amount of radiation, but I don't want to predict what the results could be. Even though a lot could happen, some of it we will see, and some we may not." I was too shy and scared to ask a lot of questions, so I just let the subject drop there. I think he knew I wasn't ready to hear any more bad news.

Next, a young man named John came to get Dawn and asked us to follow him. As he was wheeling her to the treatment room, he said, "Dawn, I'm going to take you to a room, have you lie on a table, and then a machine will dispense your treatment. Your mom and dad will watch you on a TV screen."

Dave and I stood in the room with the TV screen, as John took Dawn into the treatment room. After he got her all situated on the table and the machine up over her head, he walked out and closed the door. He ran a machine that was on a desk. He explained that this machine operated the radiation machine. My heart did flip-flops, and I grabbed Dave as I watched Dawn on the TV screen. I said to him, "I can't believe that's our little girl lying in that room under that big machine."

Dave held me and said, "She'll be all right". He was like that. He was always strong and positive in any situation. After the treatment, we went back to Dawn's room to finish packing her things to go home. With the joy that we forgot about our first experience with radiation treatments.

As Dawn got dressed, I wondered what I'd do about her head. She didn't have any hair, and she had been wearing the scarf the nurse had given her. I wanted her to look natural when we left the hospital. I wanted to forget everything that had happened there. As I thought about it, I remembered the wig that was tucked away in Dawn's stand.

Dave's sister, Violet, had brought a nice wig up to Dawn soon after the surgery, but Dawn didn't want anything to do with it. I decided the best thing to do was put it away until she was ready to accept it. She said that kids to not wear wigs.

Today I wanted her to go home looking like our little girl. I took the wig out of the stand and said to her, "Dawn, remember the wig Aunt Vi brought you. Would you like to wear it home?" I looked into Dawn's eyes as I talked and saw some resistance.

She thought for a moment and said, "I guess so."

As I put the wig on her head, I continued to watch her eyes. I seen the disgusted look on her face of neading to wear a wig, knowing she had no choice.

When she was all ready to go, I turned to Dave and commented on how nice Dawn looked. He put his arms around her and said, "Honey, you're as pretty as you always were."

She didn't seem to accept his compliment and said, "I want my own hair back."

We tried to cover up our disappointment by saying to her, "Your hair will come back soon. We'll just have to be patient."

As we left with our arms full, we said good-bye to all of Dawn's roommates. Many doctors and nurses showed up as we entered the hallway and as we wheeled Dawn down to the elevators. Dr. Alcorn was among the doctors who came to say good-bye, and he said, "Dawn, I want you to come and visit us someday when you are here for your treatment. I like to keep track of my pretty patients." She smiled at him but said nothing about coming back.

Later that evening, when we had Dawn all settled at home, Dave and I sat down and thanked God that our family was home together again. We just hadn't had time through the years to realize how much our family's being together meant to us. Now, as we sat and thought about the fact that Dawn could be taken from us, we were too scared to admit our fears and discuss them with each other. We immediately became absorbed in watching TV so Dawn would have something to do and be right in the center of the family activities.

The next couple days were great. Lori and D.J. were so glad to have us home that they were good with Dawn. They showed no signs of jealousy over the extra attention she needed. We had friends and family stopping by to offer their support and see if we needed anything.

Sunday was Easter, so Dave, Lori, and D.J. went to church, and I stayed home with Dawn. I got her all dressed in a pink slack outfit and asked her to put her wig on. She flatly said, "No, little girls don't wear wigs."

I was stunned by her quick response and the stern look on her face. I could see she was very upset with my suggestion and decided not to go any further with it then. I put the pink scarf she had been wearing back on her head and said, "Okay, you don't have to wear it today, but I think the wig looks nice."

With sadness in her voice, she said, "Only ladies wear wigs."

I tried to explain that it was all right for little girls without hair to wear wigs and to reassure her that she'd only have to wear it until her own hair came back.

The family came over to have dinner with us that day, and because it was Easter, we took a lot of pictures. After they were developed, I saw how thin Dawn was. I knew then that I had to get her to eat more. Her clothes hung on her like bags, and without hair, her face looked even thinner.

On Monday, we started our daily trips to the hospital, so Dawn could get her radiation treatments. We met and got to know some nice people there because the same patients came every day at the same time. One patient was a sixteen- year-old boy named Tom whom also had a brain tumor so came every day too. Dawn and I talked with him and his parents while we waited. She mentioned that she liked horses so that was the main topic of our conversations.

As the days passed and the routine of hospital treatments was accepted, Dawn's depression subsided. I was hurting so inside, but seeing her starting to be normal again helped me. She was able to play outside, and a homebound teacher came three times a week to help her with school work. She worked very hard with the teacher and looked forward to going back to the classroom.

I didn't talk with Dawn about her cancer and often wondered how much she understood it. I found out what a bright girl she was while she was watching TV. There was an advertisement about the statistics of cancer. After it was over, she said, "Ma, I'm a statistic, too, am I not?"

Surprised by her remark, I wasn't sure what to say, but it made me realize she understood more about cancer than I thought. I said, "Yes," and put my arms around her. I held her, saying, "You will be one of the statistics that beats cancer. You have to keep fighting and believe that God will help you through this. You do believe me, don't you?"

I looked her right in the eye as she said, "I guess so."

I made another decision about my spiritual life that day. I knew if I was going to help Dawn keep a positive attitude, I had to have one myself. I decided to start reading a devotional booklet every morning. I knew many people who said that morning devotions helped them get through each day. From the next morning on, I read a devotional guide along with my daily Bible readings. I also had a lot of questions about God's part in my life, so I decided to read the Bible all the way through. As scared as I was, I knew I had to depend a lot more on God; that meant reading His Word more and talking to Him daily.

———————•———————

Two weeks after Dawn started radiation treatments, I noticed she was stumbling around when she walked. I was sitting out in the sun when I saw her coming back home from Grandma's. She was singing as she walked. Then I saw her stumble.

"Dawn, are you okay?"

"Yes, but I'm kind of tired."

Panic set in as I wondered what could be wrong.

"You're not walking too well. Is it because you're tired?"

She responded with a slow, "I don't know."

I was so glad it was just about time for her checkup with Dr. Gracias. I had many questions I wanted to ask him. I realized that I was having a hard time, as Dawn's mother, being overly protective. Every time she got on her bike, I feared that she would fall.

Dr. Gracias was very happy with Dawn's progress when she went for her checkup. He had an answer for every question that was going through my mind.

After examining her, he said, "I'm going to stop the phenobarbital Dawn has been on since surgery. The tests show that she no longer needs it." After he explained that phenobarbital was a depressant, I realized why she was tired and stumbling all the time.

Dr. Gracias and I had quite a talk. With all the questions and fears I expressed, he gave me a lecture on caring for a child with cancer. One of the statements he made that really stood out in my mind is:"Let Dawn live life while she can. Don't hold her back from doing the things she wants to do." Afterward, I thought about that statement a lot, because of his concern for her when he said it.

When Dawn and I arrived home from the doctor's, Dave was waiting for a report. It was obvious that Dawn was in better spirits than I was. I told Dave all about my conversation with Dr. Gracias. I could tell by his reaction that he agreed with everything Dr. Gracias had said. I knew he was right, but couldn't see how I could just pretend she was again normal. All I could think about was that she could die in less than a year, and that's not normal!

Dawn made more progress after she had been off the phenobarbital a week. The treatments were going well. Her radiologist, Dr. Gillis, was pleased that she showed no side effects from the radiation. He said it's very common for patients to get very sick from the treatments. He had given her some pills in case she got sick, but she never had to use them. I kept praying every day that she wouldn't be sick after all she had been through. She was quite skinny and didn't need to lose any more weight. Before going to the hospital she weighed seventy pounds, but had shrunk to only fifty-seven.

Toward the end of April, Dawn was tired of going to the hospital every day for treatments. The day before her tenth birthday, as we sat waiting for her radiation treatment, she said, "I'm not coming here tomorrow."

Surprised, I said, "What do you mean?"

Very sternly she said, "It's my birthday."

My heart sank, thinking how I'd like to make her birthday very special but couldn't do anything about her having to come to the hospital.

I decided to ask Dr. Gillis if Dawn could skip one day, since it was her birthday. He made me see how important it was for Dawn to receive *each* daily dosage of radiation without interruption. She'd already had to skip a day the previous week because her white blood count was too low.

Dawn wasn't very happy about going back for a treatment on her birthday but got over it when walking into the waiting room. Over the door to the treatment room hung the big sign:"Happy

10th Birthday, Dawn." We were both surprised as the other patients and parents wished her happy birthday when we went into the room. Two of the patients gave her cards, each with a dollar enclosed. The message on the cards read:"Here is a dollar to buy some hay for your horse." It was good to see her face brighten with a big *thank you!*

Driving home, Dawn expressed how happy she was that it was her birthday and how nice the people at the hospital had been. I told her how proud I was that she made the best of going to the hospital and said, "Now, we'll really celebrate when we get home. I'm really happy that now you and Lori can celebrate your common birthdays together."

That year was really special, and I was determined to make the birthday celebrations for Dawn and Lori as happy as possible. The family all came over, and everyone tried to help me forget what was really on my mind. Dawn and Lori were both happy, and neither seemed affected by Dawn's illness. The birthday festivities went on just like always. I had to make myself laugh and be joyful, because I didn't want to show my true thoughts. My mind kept going over the fact that Dawn had cancer and maybe this would be the last time we would have a double-birthday celebration.

On the seventh of May, Dawn went for her last treatment. Dr. Gillis told her how proud he was of the way she handled herself through the weeks of treatment. When we got ready to go, he said, "Dawn, I won't have to see you for a month." She seemed to be pretty happy about that. She had a big wide smile snd seemed though she wanted to jump with happiness. Now that the treatments were over, we both wanted to go home and forget about cancer. Coming to the hospital every day and seeing all the other patients was a constant reminder of what cancer can do. Now, I hoped that we could get our lives back to something somewhat more normal.

The Remission Years

Dawn returned to school the last two weeks of the school year and was excited about going back. Although she didn't want to wear her wig, she didn't want to go bald either. She adjusted to wearing the wig but made it clear it wouldn't be for very long. Every time she talked about it, I remembered the words of Dr. Gillis. He had said there was a chance Dawn's hair would not grow back. He explained that the radiation could kill the cells in the brain that make the hair grow, but I kept praying that he would be wrong, thinking that Dawn wouldn't accept wearing the wig permanently.

Word got around town that Dawn wanted a horse. It didn't take long before a friend made us a deal on selling his appaloosa horse to Dawn. The idea of her riding such a large animal frightened me. Everyone was really happy for her except me. She was so little and had no strength. How could she handle such a big horse?

Dave worked with Dawn and took her for rides on the horse. She didn't like to have her dad walking with her while she was riding, but we convinced her she'd have to wait until she was stronger before she could go alone.

Dawn's dream was to ride her horse alone and go fast. She named him Skyrocket because he was fast. I lived in fear that she'd get hurt on this fast horse, but I had to keep most of those fears to myself.

When the Memorial Day Parade rolled around, Dawn wanted to be in it with her horse. She came to me and said, Mom, I'm going to ride Skyrocket in the parade tomorrow. I was surprised and, at first, thought how proud I was of her courage. After I realized what she was saying, I explained that she couldn't ride Skyrocket by herself. She got upset with me but agreed to let Dave walk along beside her.

The next day, when I saw her high on her horse with her cowboy hat and boots on, looking so happy, I cried. I found out later that a lot of other people watching the parade felt the same way. She had bounced back after a long struggle. Seeing her in the parade was a reminder of what a tough kid she was.

We had a good summer doing things together as a family. Dawn was feeling well most of the time, so we went camping as often as we could.

That July would be the fourth year that we camped with four other families out at Gun Lake. The other families and my family were all cousins, so our camp-out was like having a week-long reunion. The kids looked forward to getting together as much as the adults.

When going to the lake, we took a boat and water skis. All the kids wanted to learn how to water-ski, Dawn being no exception. Every time the boat and skis were in use, she begged me to let her ski. I couldn't consider it because of her poor coordination. I felt bad that I had to hold her back, but it was just too dangerous. Dave was willing to let her try, but—because of my protest—didn't go against my wishes. My heart would tell me to let her do what she wanted, and my good sense would tell me to be careful.

When Dawn went back to school in September, I found myself wandering around the house with too much time to dwell on her illness. The doctor bills were adding up. It seemed that every time I went to the mailbox I'd find another one. I hadn't realized so many different doctors had a part in her care. Our church had taken up a love offering to help with the medical expenses, but that went quickly. I decided I had to do something to help before I got too depressed.

I talked to Dave about getting a full-time job. He was against my working. I tried to show him that I needed to work for my mental health. I had never worked full time, and the idea was a real threat to him.

Dave didn't give me a flat no, so I decided to look for work and see what happened. I spent weeks going to restaurants and filling out applications. The more I'd look, the more depressed I became. I started feeling really down on myself because I kept getting turned down.

In early October, I went job hunting in the morning and to my uncle Wilfred's funeral in the afternoon. By the time I left the funeral home, I was so depressed that I couldn't think straight. I got in my car and headed for my friend Karen's house. Before I got there, I found my car spinning around in the middle of an intersection. I had stopped for a red light and then proceeded forward when the light was green. An eyewitness told the police that the car that hit me had run the red light.

My car was hit broadside on the driver's side, just ahead of my door. I felt very lucky not to be injured, but the car was a total wreck. I was stunned and didn't know what had happened. I knew that if I hadn't been so depressed, I would have paid better attention to the traffic. After the police officer talked to me and the driver of the other car, he took me to Karen's house.

I didn't think I was hurt in the accident, but by the time I arrived at Karen's, my head was pounding. I told her about the accident, and she felt I should go to the hospital for X-rays. I convinced her that I'd be all right, even though I wasn't really sure.

The accident occurred on Friday afternoon, and by Sunday night I was convinced that there was something wrong with me. I ached all over, and people I talked to said I should have gone for X-rays. One of my friends said I could develop a blood clot. By early Monday morning, I was fearful that I was going to die.

I woke Dave up at 4:00 a.m., saying, "Dave, take me to the hospital. I think I'm going to die." On the way, I had such terrible chest pains that I couldn't breathe. I was convinced that this was the end and said, "Dave, I'm not going to make it. I'm dying."

We went to the emergency room of Butterworth Hospital. When we got there, I could barely talk, because the pain in my chest was so great. After they started checking me out, the doctor came to me with a paper bag and told me to blow into it. He said, "You're hyperventilating." After I blew into the bag and settled down, the pain in my chest eased.

The doctor did a few tests and took X-rays. When he came to tell me the results, I was calmer and breathing normally again. The doctor said, "The X-rays show you have badly bruised muscles in your left shoulder and arm." I asked him why I had so much chest pain and trouble breathing. He said, "You were suffering from hyperthymia, which means you had an abnormal amount of mental excitability."

It was my worry about having a blood clot and not being checked out that caused my mind to work overtime. He sent me home with a prescription for muscle relaxers and orders to rest for a couple days. I left there feeling much better but foolish for letting myself get so out of control.

The next couple days, I lay on the couch and looked at the help wanted ads. I kept thinking about our wrecked car and how much harder it would be now to look for a job. Dave said the accident could be a sign that I shouldn't go to work, but I couldn't go along with that theory. When I prayed, I continued to praise God for saving me from serious injuries and asked Him to guide me in my job search.

Finally the day came; I applied for work as a cashier at Haan's Foods, a grocery store. It was seventeen miles away from home, but I was determined.

Five days later I was called in for an interview. The manager was satisfied with me but was concerned about my living so far away. I convinced him that it wouldn't be a problem and I'd be dependable. He said I could have the job at a starting pay of $2.10 per hour, forty hours a week with paid holidays.

I was happy to get the job, but on the way home, I wondered how I'd tell Dave about the long hours and low pay. The more I thought about it, the more I worried about the change in lifestyle for our family. Dave wasn't happy when I told him about the job but agreed to let me work everything out.

There were lots of adjustments to be made by all of us, but I was determined to make it work. Working got me out of the house and gave me some money to help with the mounting bills.

Dawn seemed to be doing really well in school. She even joined the band and started playing a clarinet, which was exciting for her. She worked very hard on her studies, coming home every night and doing homework without me reminding her. I was so pleased that she was adjusting back to a normal childhood.

I thought things were going well at school for Dawn until one day on my day off she had come home crying. I asked her what was wrong. Throwing her books on the table, she said,

"I fell at school, and my wig came off. The kids all laughed at me."

To console her, I took her in my arms and said, "Dawn, I'm so sorry the kids were mean."

Shouting back at me, she said, "I'm not going back!"

I felt bad for her but knew that would happen sooner or later. Kids didn't realize the harm of teasing. We continued talking about her wig and school for she knew she had to go back and forget the mean remarks. I wanted to go to school and tell kids to lay off but knew she had to handle it herself.

When Christmas rolled around, I felt so thankful and happy. While watching the excitement of our children as they opened their gifts, I wondered how long this family would be together and happy. *Dawn was doing well, but how long would it last?* I got angry with myself for even asking that question. *Oh, please, Lord, forgive me for doubting that she'll be all right*, I prayed. Our family caught the real spirit of Christmas this year, because of the renewed love we had for Jesus and His love.

On New Year's Eve, as Dave and I welcomed in 1976, we asked God to make the New Year better. We wanted to forget the cancer and all the events that led up to it. Living with the idea that the cancer could come back was so hard to think about, yet I did. I wanted someone to reassure me that Dawn would never have it again, but that person could not be found.

When spring came, we looked forward to summer with the kids out of school and decided to make advance plans for a family vacation. Dave's sister, Virginia, lived in Mississippi. We'd never been south with the kids, so we decided to visit. When we told the kids about the trip with our camper, they were all excited. We decided to stop in Tennessee at Opryland Park along the way. As the time approached for our trip, I let fear creep into my happiness, wondering what we'd do if Dawn got sick while we were gone and needed her doctor. We had never gone on a trip so far away from home. What if something were to happen along the way?

We left on our trip the second week in June. Traveling with the kids in the camper was enjoyable. Our day at Opryland Park was tiring but fun. Because Dawn tired easily the kids went on the rides between some music shows. When the park closed we went back to the camper. We then munched on goodies while talking and laughing about the fun we had. I wanted to take those moments and hold them tight The next three days were spent fishing, sightseeing, and resting in Mississippi with Dave's sister and husband. It was nice to be away from home and from the everyday problems.

We almost forgot Dawn had a problem until the day she had a slight seizure. It didn't really amount to much; she stared and had a hard time talking. Though it didn't last long, it shook us up and reminded me that I had better watch her medication. I checked her Dilantin pills and found that she had missed one two days in a row. With all the fun we were having, we forgot about the Dilantin. She usually takes her pill every morning after breakfast. I felt guilty when I realized I had forgotten them.

The rest of the trip went fast. We made a stop in Memphis and rode the Mississippi riverboat then on to Chicago to tour the Museum of Science and Industry. The trip was taking its toll on Dawn. We didn't get through much of the museum before she started complaining about being too tired to walk. By the time we arrived home the next day, Father's Day, we were all tired and cross.

That night when I said my prayers, I thanked God for our safe trip and the good time we had. I was so thankful that we had the chance to take the trip and show the kids another part of the country.

As the summer went on, I found Dawn in the house more than she was outside. I asked her why she spent so much time inside, and she said, "There is nothing to do." I noticed she wasn't playing very much with kids her age. They were all so active while she tired so quickly. She tried to ride her bike, but even that was getting hard.

A year ago Dave and I had joined a group called "Living with Cancer," a support group for parents of a child with cancer.

The cancer group planned a picnic in August for all the families. My kids were eager to go when they learned that the picnic would be at a home with a swimming pool. They had met kids from other families at a previous party in December.

We all decided to go to the picnic. When we got there, people were swimming already. At first Dawn didn't want to take her wig off. When she finally did, she jumped immediately into the pool, finding she was not the only child there with hair loss; there were several.

The Grand Rapids Press came to take pictures. They wanted to do a story on our group—the only cancer support group in that part of Michigan.

I didn't realize that the press took a picture of Dawn and me and was startled a couple days later when a coworker showed me such a picture on the front page of the"Flair" section. Several people at work kidded me about being a celebrity. I surely didn't feel like a celebrity or that having a child with cancer was a desirable way to get my picture in the paper.

When I looked at the pictures of the cancer families in the paper, I thought about all the heartache and worry that goes with having a child with cancer. I talked to a mother at the picnic who said her twelve-year-old son was taking chemotherapy but had refused to take any more treatments. He had had *enough* of them. Tumors were throughout his body and treatments weren't helping anymore. She said it had been a hard decision to make but felt he had the right to make it. I knew by our conversation that she and her son had a lot of faith. I wondered if I'd be able to let Dawn make a decision like that?

In September, before the kids started back to school, I bought them some new clothes. For Dawn, part of the wardrobe was a new wig. She didn't like picking one out, but the one she had looked rather used. After shopping several places, we finally found one that could be styled to suit her. She looked quite cute when the stylist finished with it. When we left the salon, Dawn asked, "Mom, when is my own hair coming back?"

I was afraid to answer that, because I knew by now that it probably was not going to. I gently tried to explain that her hair might never come back."We'll just have to keep praying about it," I said.

Everything went well the first couple months of school. Dawn was very happy to be in sixth grade with one of her friends who she hadn't been with the last couple years. This girlfriend, whose name was also Dawn Marie Smith, was a friend from her earlier childhood years.

Dawn enjoyed being with the other Dawn again and talked with her often.

As time went on, I noticed Dawn was spending a lot of time after school with homework. She would sit at the table some nights for hours. Many times I would try to get her to put away the books. When she did, she'd get out her clarinet.

Since joining the band the year before, she had taken her practicing very seriously. I had a sudden realization that homework and playing the clarinet were becoming very difficult for her. I talked to her about it, but she denied having trouble.

I was very concerned that Dawn had to spend so much time with her schoolwork. I didn't feel she should work all day and night, too. Whenever I'd try to pull her away, she'd get mad and shout, "I have to get this done!" I admired her dedication, but I was still troubled. I began to think about the radiation she had had more than a year ago and wondered if it had damaged her learning ability. Oh, what a frightening thought!

I was also having problems of my own at this time. My left leg was so painful that I could hardly walk. It seemed to be around the knee area. It felt like there was a bump behind my knee. When I couldn't stand it at work, I went to a doctor. He told me I had a baker's cyst and to wrap my leg in a bandage during the day for three weeks and then come back.

As the weeks passed, my depression and pain got worse. While going to several doctors over the next few months, each one gave me a different opinion and treatment. I became so confused that I decided not to do anything.

I was in such pain that I was always tired and grouchy after work. Dave and I started quarreling over silly things. I wasn't happy at work or home. At work my leg hurt, and at home I had to face Dawn's problems.

I had hoped that 1977 would be a better year, but new problems kept coming. Dawn complained about headaches so much that on February 25th I took her to the hospital for an EEG. It turned out to be okay, and my mind was relieved. Soon after Dawn had the EEG, I talked to one of her teachers at school. She said Dawn had trouble falling on the stairs a lot. The stairways were crowded, and when the kids change classes, Dawn was shoved in the process. She lost her balance and fell.

Learning of Dawn's falls was a shock to me. When I questioned her about it, she said, "The kids try to go too fast." I wondered why she hadn't told me about it, yet I knew she was trying hard to be normal and didn't want me to worry. I did worry, though. If she kept falling, sooner or later she'd get hurt.

She still sat at the table at night with her books, not ready to accept the fact that she wasn't able to get the good grades of earlier years. It was hard for me, too. I wanted very much for her to be able to retain that ability. Watching her struggle so hard was difficult for me to accept.

As I struggled with my pain and Dawn's problems, I found myself pulling away from our church. I read my devotions every day and prayed, but when it came to attending church on Sunday, I felt lost. Our church is active, and I'd always been a part of the activity. I didn't know how to handle my depression or ask for help. I tried talking to Reverend Bud but never gave him a chance to get down to what was really bothering me. I would go to church on Sunday morning and expect Reverend Bud and everyone else to be able to read my mind. I cried on the inside and laughed on the outside. I worried about Dawn to the point where my own health was failing.

I quit going to church for a few weeks, thinking if I quit going people would wonder why. I talked Dave into going to another church. I was reaching out but didn't know how to do it. When praying I asked God to understand my anxiety but didn't get the comfort I looked for. After several weeks of frustration and a talk with Reverend Bud, we went back to our church. I quit exppecting the church family to know my feelings. A few families from the cancer group and I were counseled by a psycholgist Doug Ellis. One time I was so uptight and poured out my feelings to the group. Doug, as he wanted to be called, handled it very well. I talked about Dawn's falling at school and her constant studying at home. I admitted that I didn't feel qualified to handle her condition. That night Doug had me face up to the fact that I and no one else would look after her needs.

I had felt for some time that Dawn would have to change schools. She couldn't continue the fast pace at the middle school. After I talked to several of her teachers and found she was doing poorly, I knew it was time. She was also having such a hard time in band trying to play her clarinet that the other kids noticed her lack of skill. She just didn't have the strength to blow the clarinet.

I had already talked to the school guidance counselor once about Dawn. His theory was to give her easy classes and let her slide by. He didn't feel she needed an education because of her being a cancer patient. On the other hand, Doug pointed out that Dawn wanted an education, and she should be placed in a school where there was special education available for kids with handicaps. I went to the guidance counselor again and this time told him what I wanted for her. We talked quite a while, and upon leaving I felt good about how I had presented Dawn's needs. The counselor agreed to check into another school setting for next fall. I made up my mind then that she wouldn't go back to such a school if she had to compete with stairs, academic load, and fast-paced life of the middle school. My heart didn't want to admit her failing abilities, but my mind had known for some time that the radiation damage was showing up.

As time went on and Dawn kept struggling, I continued to build up anxiety. One day, I received a call at work from my mom. I heard my name over the intercom, "Marilyn, telephone, line two," I panicked. I raced to the office, picked up the phone, and heard my mother say, "Marilyn, Dawn blacked out at school and fell." I went right home, with fear building. Mom had said Dawn was all right but I had to see for myself. I found Dawn lying on Mom's couch with a big bump on her head and a black eye. I was frightened and angery, mad at the school, as if it was their fault, and at myself for not being home when she needed me. Dawn recovered from her fall and I got worse. The pain in my leg, back and headaches were more frequent. I was sent for X-rays on my back which showed I had scoliosis. Dave didn't know how to cope with me anymore. He heard my complaints and tried to be supportive, but he too was getting frustrated.

When school let out for the summer and Dawn didn't have homework, I thought she'd spend time enjoying herself instead of studying. After work I'd come home to find the same scene I had found the previous summer. She'd be lying around in the house. She just didn't seem to have a lot of strength. Her weight and size were still the same as the year before.

Dawn was due for another checkup with her radiologist, Dr. Gillis. I asked him about my fears. He confirmed that we were seeing radiation damage. Dawn was not growing much, and her learning abilities were deteriorating. I didn't let him know how much that news upset me, but by the time we got home, my brain was ready to explode.

I told Dave about Dawn's checkup. He tried to calm me by saying, "We knew this was a possibility, didn't we?"

I asked why so many times. I kept reading the Scriptures looking for answers. Why does our child have to be different? God's Word didn't tell me why Dawn had to have these problems, but I did hear God telling me to trust and have faith. Some people believe that God has a plan for our lives and that whatever happens is part of His will. I did not believe that God would will a small child to suffer radiation damage because of having cancer.

Everything I've read in the Bible leads me to believe that He wants us to have abundant life, but because life has its problems, that can't always happen. I do believe that, if we have faith in God's love, He'll help us handle anything that is put before us.

The next day my head felt better, and I went back to work. I tried to get involved in my work, so I could forget about the thoughts that had been going through my mind. I had a lot of plans to make for Dawn's schooling in the fall, so I had to straighten myself up.

Over the Fourth of July, Dave and I decided to take a four-day trip to Niagara Falls with our friends Sandy and Jim. We had never left our children but felt we needed to be by ourselves. When our family and friends found out we wanted to take the trip, they offered to watch the kids.

The rest of the summer went by with Lori and D.J. having their normal fun. Dawn kept trying but struggled just to ride her bike. Lori and Dawn both went to our church camp. Dawn was excited when she went to camp, but when Dave picked her up, she couldn't get home fast enough.

Before Dawn went to bed that night, she took a bath. I walked into the bathroom just as she was getting out of the tub. I looked at her and gasped, "Dawn, what happened to you?"

I was horrified at the bruises all over her thin body.

She realized the shock I felt and said, "I knew you were going to do that."

She told me she had fallen several times because of the ruts in the woods at camp.

As usual, Dawn healed and kept going as if nothing had happened. Her determination was such an inspiration to me, to other people, too. My sister Barb gave me a poem written by her husband Wally, who lives with all four limbs paralyzed:

Dawn

Dawn is the glimmering hope of a brand new day.
Dawn's shining existence makes the darkness slip away.
Dawn's presence in summer causes the birds to sing.
Dawn sheds light and loveliness on everything.
Dawn begins a warmth to last the whole day through.
Dawn relieves the hard nights, for she has been there, too.
Dawn is a young girl to me, not the rising sun.

Dawn, like the sun, gives strength and hope to everyone.
Dawn is a vibrant witness to a living God above.
Dawn in every way is within the power of His love.
So, if this proud old uncle ever feels all hope is gone;
All he has to do is look into the shining eyes of Dawn.

I was extremely touched after reading the poem. Wally had put into beautiful words some of the things I felt. Dawn was an inspiration to me, but to find out she was an inspiration to Wally was a revelation. He had been paralyzed for eleven years. I hugged Barb and asked her to tell Wally that the poem meant a lot to me. She and Wally had written it after watching and talking to Dawn. She understood her condition and was determined to overcome it.

I talked with God, asking Him to help me reach a stage of acceptance of Dawn's disabilities and my knee pain. I had expected doctors to help me when I should have been asking for God's. I managed to get through the rest of the summer by constant communication with God through prayer and by keeping busy.

Facing the Changes

When September rolled around and it was time for school to start, I wondered what I should do about Dawn going back. She was excited about seventh grade and marching with the band. We hadn't looked into sending her to another school, there were none in the area where she could go so Dave and I decided to let her try the old school one more year. When I asked her about changing schools, she said, "Mom, I don't want to leave my friends."

"But Dawn, what about the stairs? You fell down so much last year."

"I'll be more careful."

I didn't really want her to leave her home, her school, or her friends either, but I found out that's what she'd have to do. There was no special program at our school.

The week before school started, I took the kids shopping with the idea of making it a fun day. Lori and D.J. had to have several new outfits, because they had grown so much. When Dawn tried on new slacks, I was again faced with the fact that she hadn't grown any in the past year. Because she hadn't grown since fifth grade, she really didn't need many new clothes. The idea of her not growing was so scary, and seeing her try on the same size clothes, while the other two kids had to get larger sizes, was just one more depressing reminder.

After looking at clothes, we went to the wig department to look them over. When I approached Dawn about buying a new wig, she flatly said, "No, I don't want one." Lori and I both tried to convince her, but she still refused. We tried to show her how much nicer the new ones looked compared to hers, but that didn't matter. Almost in tears, she finally said, "Mom, I don't want to have a different hairstyle when I go back to school. The kids at school will tease me."

Oh, I thought, *the truth finally comes out.* Dawn had always been self-conscious about having to wear a wig. I knew she was right about being teased, so I decided to give in. The one she was wearing looked bad, but it just wasn't worth hurting her anymore. I left the store feeling very frustrated about the whole shopping trip.

———•———

Dawn got along pretty well in school the first couple of months. The counselor arranged her schedule so she had easy subjects, and she was in the marching band.

As time went on, it became harder to cope with Dawn's learning disabilities and the pain in my knee. Just like last year, she started coming home with homework she couldn't handle. She tried to do book reports, which were just about impossible. Her mind didn't seem to comprehend anything she read. When she got her first report card and saw her grades were poor, she got so upset she threw it across the room. I said, "Dawn, don't worry about your grades; you're trying hard enough."

"No, I'm not!" she said, stomping across the room to the couch to lie down. I tried to comfort and reassure her, but it didn't seem to help.

I went to the hospital, as an outpatient, in late October to have a needle test done on my knee. My mother went along with me that day to drive me home. On the way back, I asked her what the doctor had said."He really didn't say much other than the fact that he found some particles floating around," she answered."He wants you to go to his office in a week to talk over the test." I was disappointed that he hadn't told her more. It made me feel very down. When walking into the house, I was so withdrawn that I headed right for the couch. Dave and the kids were around but didn't notice my depressed look right away. Dawn was the first to notice my crying. She said, "What's the matter, Ma?" I told her I didn't feel good, so she put her arms around me. It wasn't long before Dave came in and wanted to know what the doctor said. After I told him what was said he came back with,"You have to accept what the doctor said. You're gotten more depressed by going to so many doctors. There'll all given you a different opinion." I knew he was right.

When I went back to the doctor's office a week later, I was excited about getting some answers to my knee problems, but was a nervous wreck while waiting for the doctor to come into the examining room. I stared around the room, thinking about all the times I'd sat waiting for a doctor to give me some answers to my knee problems. I stared around the room, thinking about all the times I'd sat waiting for a doctor to give me some answers.

When the doctor finally did come in, I was afraid of what he was going to say. After greeting me, he went on to tell me that I had a lot of inflammation in the knee and that there were also particles floating around. He said, "There isn't too much that can be done. Take a lot of aspirin for the inflammation, and keep your weight where it is. If you want, someday surgery could be done to scrape off some of the particles. I wouldn't recommend it now, though."

I didn't know what questions to ask, so when I left there, I didn't feel that I had found out a whole lot. As a result of feeling so depressed, I sat in the car and stared for a while before I could start home. Driving through the city, I barely paid attention to the lights. My mind was deep in thought, reviewing what the doctor had just told me. I didn't feel any closer to finding out why my knee ached so badly. Tears started rolling as I asked why. There was a feeling of being let down and deserted. What was I to tell Dave? I felt he was getting discouraged with me because of all my doctor visits about the same problem. On the way home my mind was in such a depressed state that I almost drove into a ditch. The worst part was that I didn't care. I pulled the car away and the rest of the way home kept asking God to help me, believing He knew how I was feeling. "Please, God, don't let me feel this way."

The rest of the year was pretty rocky for our family. Dawn kept having problems at school, and when she came home, she would sit in pure frustration, trying to do her homework. Every time I tried to talk to her about it, she got mad.

My knee pain didn't get any better, and as a result of trying to cope with that, I started having other health problems. There was still very much depression, despite my Bible reading. Dave was having a hard time dealing with me, so we kept arguing over almost everything. Another thing I noticed was that DJ was developing all kinds of ailments. I knew his big problem was wanting attention ever since Dawn had been in the hospital 2 years ago, he had come off sick or hurt quite often. We never knew when to take his complaint seriously. Most of the time I tried to give him the attention he wanted and downplay his complaint. Lori seemed to be the only one who had adjusted and had a normal routine.

When the old year neared its end, Dave and I again looked forward to the new year. On New Year's Eve we said to each other, "I hope 1978 will be a better year." We didn't think it could get much worse. It wasn't long into the new year when things started happening. I let my nerves get so bad that I went to our family doctor in Wayland for a complete physical. I had found blood in my stool which immediately started me imagining that I had all kinds of things wrong with me. When I told Dr. Hayden about all my problem, he checked me very carefully doing many minor test. He told me that I had large cyst in my breast, inflammation in my knee, and very bad nerves. He went on to say that if I could find out for sure what was wrong with my knee it would help with my nerves. The reason I was having so much pain and blood in the stool was because of anxiety.

Before I left that day, he talked to me a lot about Dawn. I guess he figured out that she was much of my anxiety. I felt he was someone that really cared about what I was going through. He made an appointment for me to see a specialist who deals with knee problems but couldn't get me in until April. It was shocking that I'd have to wait so long but then remembered I had said just a few months earlier that I wouldn't go to a doctor again about my knee.

As time went on, I started developing problems at work. I was very jumpy and down on my boss, thinking he was not being fair to me with some of the work he was having *me* do. Now, I realize the reason for not getting along with people at work was because of the stress I felt at home. On the way home at night, I daydreamed about running off. So many times as I drove down the expressway toward home I had the urge just to drive on, not really knowing where I'd go. I knew God would not want me to run off and leave my family so I faced reality and got off at the right exit.

In March, Lori fet sick with strap infection, which kept her in bed with a fever for days. About the same time, Dawn started complaining about stomachaches. Her complaining got so bad that Dr. Gracias wanted her admitted to the hospital for tests.

I was very apprehensive about taking Dawn to the hospital but realized there could be a problem. I just hoped and prayed that the stomachaches wouldn't be associated with the brain tumor she had three years ago.

After a week of tests and a CAT scan, there was no evidence of either a tumor or shunt failure. Dr. Gracias had told us when he put a shunt in Dawn that there would always be the possibility of it plugging up.

I was very relieved to find that Dawn had no other serious problems but felt very depressed about not finding out why she had stomachaches. I began to wonder if she wasn't suffering from anxiety over schoolwork.

I went to school and found out from Dawn's teachers that she was trying hard with her schoolwork. The band director Mr

Dunsmore said anytime Dawn had to do a solo that was very hard for her but the other kids seemed understanding about her mistakes.

Dawn was taking classes at church so she could be confirmed in the church. Reverend Bud called me one day and asked if Dawn could go to Chicago overnight with the confirmation class. My first thought was to say no; I didn't think she'd be able to keep up. Lori had taken the same trip two years ago with her class, so I knew they got pretty tired before they returned home. I told him I'd talk it over with Dave.

After Dave and I discussed the pros and cons about letting her go, he convinced me that it would be unfair to hold her back because of my fear.

I was very happy the day Dawn came home so bubbly about her experiences in Chicago. She couldn't wait to tell her father and me all about it. She was obviously very tired, but that I expected. I said a prayer that night in thanks to God for her coming home safe and happy.

We experienced a very high point the day Dawn was confirmed in our church. She looked so little standing beside the other kids, but I was very proud of her. She was very proud of herself, too. She said to me, "Mom, I'm a member of this church now, too." I was so happy that I could not stop huging and kissing her. It was exciting to have her care about being a member of God's Church.

Right after reaching a high point I went back down so low that I again wanted to escape. The day I went to see Dr. Hayden was one when I was feeling like that. He could tell when he walked into the examining room that I was on a downer. He explained that the X-ray showed I have degenerative osteoarthritis which is inherited. I asked him why the other doctors hadn't explained it to me like that. I was mad when he said, "No doctor who doesn't know you will tell you because of your job." He said that most doctors stay away from any case that could be job-related. He seemed to think that my job was aggravating my arthritis. He said a lot of people want to go on compensation because of arthritis pain.

The more he told me the madder I got, and I said to him, "I'm not the type to lie around. I have no intention of leaving my job." He said I would have to take high dosages of aspirin, which the other doctors had told me also, and rest my knee as much as possible. After telling him I was a very busy person and wondered how there would be time, he quickly said, "Take the time if you want some relief from the pain."

My mind was mixed up when I left Dr. Hayden's that day, but I was thankful that he was truthful with me but furious about having gone to so many other doctors who gave me the runaround. Realizing this added more fuel to my depression, it was difficult to forget that I had spent so much time and money the last couple years only to find out now that I have a chronic disease for which there is no cure.

It seemed as though things weren't going very well for Dawn or for me lately. I got a call a couple times about Dawn's falling at school. The second call really scared me. She fell down the longest flight of stairs in the school.

I came home from work and found her on our couch, all bruised up and with a black eye. She looked terrible. I tried to ask her what had happened, but she couldn't remember.

Three days after Dawn's fall, Mom had to bring her home from school two days in a row because of dizziness. On the second day, when I came home and found she had come from school bruised again, I was furious. I made up my mind to pull her out of middle school, vowing she wouldn't go back in the fall. She was trying too hard to keep up with the fast pace of school.

I went to the school counselor again, but this time I told him about my plans to keep Dawn out of school next fall, saying we wouldn't send her to school until they found a place for her to go that didn't have steps to climb. I wanted her in a special class so she wouldn't have to function in a normal class routine. After having watched her struggle again for another year, it was obvious that it was time to change schools.

I got some good advice from Dawn's doctors and other parents who had kids with special needs. They told me a lot about the special education laws. The point emphasized was that I'd have to stand up for Dawn's rights, and that was something I was not used to doing.

Every time I turned around that spring, there was a new thing to be dealt with. Dawn developed a bad rash on her upper lip. At first I didn't think much of it and figured it would go away. Then after several weeks of the rash, she started in again complaining of headaches and dizziness.

My mind was overwhelmed. My headachae and upset stomach returned. I did not stop thinking about Dawn's continued complaints. Every time I tried to talk to Dave about it, he'd tell me I worried too much.

I decided to take Dawn to Dr. Hayden to check the rash she had. He said she had impetigo and gave her a shot of penicillin. I thought that would clear it up and be the end of it, but that expectation was wrong.

A few days later, Dawn got up, scratching herself all over. She came into the kitchen and said, "Mom, I itch terrible. There is more rash all over me."

I checked her all over, not wanting to believe it. I took her back to Dr. Hayden that day. He said, "The rash looks like a reaction to something." After many questions and a couple tests, he decided she was having a reaction to the penicillin he gave her. He said that in the future, she shouldn't be treated with penicillin. We found out many years earlier that Dave was allergic to penicillin and now Dawn was, too.

After several weeks Dawn's rash finally healed up, but I found myself in a bad mood most of the time. I kept worrying about her. I didn't dare share my worries with anyone, because everyone which included family, church friends even Dave kept saying"don't worry." They could all see I was depressed a lot, so apparently that was their way of helping me cope.

Out of desperation I went back to Dr. Hayden again. He was so nice to me, spending a lot of time listening to my troubles. He said I showed signs of severe depression. He did tests to find out how bad it really was. I, of course, was aware of the depression but kept thinking it would go away.

A couple of weeks later, when the test results were back, Dr. Hayden called me to his office. He said, "Marilyn, I want you to see a psychiatrist." I was stunned by his words. I thought of myself as being worried not depressed. To me ther was a difference. He said the tests showed that I was suffering from depression severe enough to affect my health.

I decided to try going to a county psychologist who came to Wayland once a week to see people in this area. After two sessions with him, that appeared to be a mistake. He didn't seem to be very interested in my real problems. I watched his face and most of the time I talked he looked down at his watch. I took as he was waiting for my hour with him to be over instead of listening to what I had said.

I told him about Dawn and my problems with arthritis pain. His answers were cut-and-dried. He said in a cold robotic tone, "You have to accept the fact that Dawn may die because of her illness." It was hard to believe he said that. I bocked it out thinking he was being to cold. I didn't want to think about such a thing happening. Now he was saying that it was necessary to be ready for that to happen any time. I just couldn't go along with that.

When it came to my arthritis, he wanted me to change jobs. Even after my explanation that I liked my job and wasn't qualified for anything else, it didn't seem to make any difference; he still kept saying I'd have to change jobs. When it came to my job he told me simply to change even though I said I enjoyed it and was not qualified for something else.

The second time I talked to him he again looked at his watch a lot. After that, I decided there was no point in going back.

The next few days I was so down that my prayers reflected my moods. My prayers were, "Lord, is there any hope for me? Please don't give up on me." Because of my moodiness around the house, Dave gave up trying to help me. I was really thinking God would, too. The more I read my Bible, the greater the expectation for answers to come quickly. But there just weren't any.

One bright spot appeared in those gloomy days when Dave and I were asked to work on the local radio station on St. Jude's Radio-thon. A spokesman from St. Jude's came to our cancer group and asked for volunteers. We spent a few hours at the station with other parents of cancer children, answering the telephone. It was a great feeling to be a part of raising money for such a worthy cause. After that weekend of talking so much about the suffering of other children, I took a different outlook for a while on my problems.

My mood swings were so unpredictable that my family never knew what to expect when I'd come home from work. I felt like life had cheated Dawn out of a normal childhood and me out of a healthy daughter. I began to think the pain in my leg was the devil trying to trick me into hating God because of my problems. Some days, it appeared the devil won.

The doctor gave me Valium but I only took it on days I felt like a bear. I hadn't wanted to become dependent on them

We went camping a few times. The kids liked camping, and Dawn seemed to get along okay.

Our third camping trip was to Gun Lake with our cousins. During the last days of camp-out, Dawn started sleeping a lot. I didn't think too much about it until one evening I went into the camper to check on her and noticed the side of her head looked red. I examined her head and neck. The redness seemed to be in the area of her shunt.

My cousin Jo Ann, who is a nurse, thought there was reason to be concerned. She felt, as I did, that there could be some infection around the shunt.

After Dave and I discussed what to do, we decided that we'd take her to Dr. Hayden in Wayland. Dr. Hayden looked Dawn over very carefully noticing the rash on her neck. He asked me a lot of questions one of which was how long she had it. I told him she had been scraching the area since having poisen ivy in late May. I could tell by the worried look on his face that he was very concerned about her. He wanted to know Dr. Gracias's phone number and went right to the phone and called him.

When he came back, my heart skipped a beat as he said, "Dr. Gracias wants you to take Dawn down to Butterworth Emergency."

"Why?" I asked.

"He wants to check her. There is a possibility that her shunt is infected."

After telling Dave that we had to take Dawn to the hospital, I fell apart and cried when telling Dave we had to take Dawn to the hospital. I could not response when he tried comforting me because of thinking about what that meant. Dawn was so sleepy that she didn't even ask questions about what was happening.

It seemed as if we sat in the emergency waiting room for hours before Dr. Gracias got there. When arriving into the room, it didn't take him long to decide what had to be done. He looked at us and said, "Dawn's shunt is infected, and it must come out immediately." He then explained the details of the surgery and why it had to be done right away which sounded very scary. He made a point of saying he'ed been surprised the shunt worked as long as it did before becoming infected. He went on to say it's quite common for them to plug up and when they did it caused pressure on the brain. The pressure comes from backed-up fluid, which could cause death if not released.

Dr. Gracias told us he was supposed to be on vacation, but he would do the surgery. He said he was not going to put another shunt in if her brain could get along without it. He felt there was a possibility that she may not have to have another one. The only way to find that out was to let her go a couple days without one. After Dr. Gracias explained everything, I felt drained. What I thought was so simple yesterday seemed so dreadful now. As Dawn was swiftly taken off and prepared for surgery, I could not help but think of how brave she was. She didn't seem at all scared, or possibly she was just too sick to care. Holding onto Dave, I told him how scared I was. The risks of surgery must be mentioned every time it's done so was upset.

The surgical waiting room was empty, unlike the last time Dawn had surgery. I felt the stillness of the room as soon as we walked in. It was not a sorce of comfort but one of loneness. We sat down, not saying a word for quite some time. The memories of Dawn's prior surgery were vivid in my mind. I felt so tense as the flashbacks of the past surgery were hard to escape.

After three hours, Dr. Gracias came in and said, "The surgery went fine."

"What will happen if she can't get along without one?" I asked.

"The fluid will increase on the brain, and she'll become unresponsive. We'll have to go in there and put a new one in as quickly as we took the old one out. We'll put her in the intensive care unit until we know for sure within thirty-two hours." I did not absorb much of his explaination of the dangers of brain infection because of hearing yet another chance of surgery.

Dr. Gracias explained all the dangers of brain infection, but I didn't absorb much. Just hearing that there could be further surgery scared me. He was on vacation but said he could be reached at home. Dawn is to be cared for by his partner, Dr. John. I knew he had a right to a vacation, but it made me nervous to think someone else might have to operate on Dawn.

It seemed like hours before Dawn was brought back to the intensive care unit in pediatrics. Some of the nurses remembered her and were eager to hear how she had been doing the last three years. Dr. Gracias had said I could stay overnight, so the nurses tried to make me comfortable.

Dawn didn't wake up much. I stayed and slept in a chair by her bed. I tried to pray instead of worrying but worried anyway.

Dawn was more alert the next day but didn't say much. I asked her if she was scared and she said no. I explained the surgery to her, trying to reassure her that she'd be okay.

That evening Dave said he'd stay with Dawn. He said I looked tired and wanted me to get some sleep. "You look tired," he said. "You need to get some sleep." After much argument, I finally agreed to go home, though I hated leaving her. Mom and Dad were there and offered to take me and bring me back in the morning. Though I did not get much sleep that night I was glad the decision was made that I go home, because Lori and D. J. were eager to see me. I told them about the surgery and let them know that Dawn would need me at the hospital for a few days. Lori seemed to understand, but D. J. looked disappointed. I reassured him that I wouldn't be away from him that long.

The next morning at the hospital, I found Dave asleep on the couch in the lobby so I woke him up. I said, "How was Dawn's night? "Pretty good, She slept most of the time."

Mom and Dad had went in to see her while Dave and I talked. When they came out, Dave left with them. I went into Dawn's room expecting to talk to her. It was 8:00 a.m., and I figured she'd be waking up. After I kissed her, she didn't respond to my touch. I started moving her around and panic struck me when she still didn't respond. Barb, Dawn's nurse, said she'd call Dr. John. I asked her if Dawn's unresponsiveness meant that she needed a shunt. She tried to reassure me that Dawn was all right, but the concern in her eyes was noticeable.

Soon after Barb left the room, Dawn's pediatrician, Dr. Bakker, came in. I filled him in on what had happened to Dawn over the weekend. He examined her and said, "I think you're right about Dawn's condition. She shows signs of pressure." He left the room to talk to the head nurse.

I heard him ask the nurse if Dr. John had been in to see Dawn. She said he hadn't and they couldn't seem to page him down. After they discussed Dawn's condition, Dr. Bakker came back in and told me he had ordered a CAT scan. He said that by the time Dawn went for a CAT scan and came back, Dr. John would probably be available to read it. He told me not to worry and left.

The ambulance came for Dawn, and her nurse, Barb, went with her a few blocks away to the Medical Arts Building. As the ambulance left, I felt overwhelming fear. My body started tencing up and so did the headache. Her condition was exactly like Dr. Gracias had described. I remembered him saying a shunt might have to be put back in as quickly as it had been taken out.

I tried to relax, knowing it would be awhile before Dawn returned.

After a long wait, Dawn was brought back. I was shocked by the sight of her forehead. It looked so swollen. I asked Barb about it, and she said it could be from the pressure. She was trying to contact Dr. John to read the scan.

I paced back and forth from Dawn's bed and down the hall. I was jumpy praying out loud as if to be sure God herd me, "Please, Lord, bring Dawn's doctor here before it is too late."

My friend Herta was due to come at 12:30 p.m. for lunch. By the time she arrived at 12:45 p.m., I was a total wreck. When I saw her outside the ICU door, I told her what had happened. She said, "You should call Dr. Gracias." I told her I was reluctant because he was on vacation.

Just as I was preparing to call Dr. Gracias, I saw him come in."Dr. Gracias," I said, "something is wrong with Dawn." He went to her bed and tried to get her to respond with no results.

He turned and asked, "How long has she been like this?"

"Since this morning at eight," I said.

He went out and talked to the head nurse. I could see that he was very upset. He was talking loudly and it seemed to me he got after the nurse for not calling him. I also saw him look at Dawn's CAT scan and throw it down.

When he came back in, he said, "Dawn has to have another shunt put in right away. The CAT scan shows there is a lot of pressure."

He explained how he had been very restless all morning, not knowing why. He couldn't understand why he was thinking about his patients instead of enjoying his vacation. He got so restless that he told his wife he was going to the hospital. On the way, he wondered which patient to check first, because several were critical. By the time he arrived, he had decided to see Dawn. I told him I was thankful and that I had been praying for someone to help her.

After he left to prepare for surgery, I sat a few minutes and thanked God that He answered my prayers by sending Dr. Gracias. I was so releaved that he was there but worried it might be to late.

I called Dave and told him what had happened. He said he'd be right there so Herta stayed helping to calm my nerves. I then prayed that the shunt could be put back in.

When Dave arrived, it was time to go to the surgical waiting room for the third time.

It seemed unfair for Dawn to go through that again.

After a few tense hours, Dr. Gracias returned and said, "The surgery went well. Dawn will be all right." I was relieved until he told us about the danger of the new shunt getting infected because of the infection still present in the brain. After Dr. Gracias left, I expressed my fear to Dave. He tried to comfort me, but it didn't seem to help much.

Dawn was back in intensive care in pediatrics and placed in the same room. The night went slowly. I tried to sleep in a chair by Dawn's bed, but it was very uncomfortable. However, Dawn did very well. Her vitals stayed stable, and she slept all night.

I could hardly wait for her to wake up so I could talk to her. My excitement turned into disappointment when she awakened.

She just stared right through me. She seemed angry for I had seen that look of blank stare so many times before. Her nurse, Barb, brought in a liquid breakfast, but she wouldn't touch it. I tried to talk to her, but she wouldn't listen. She just turned her head away as if to say she did not want to hear my words anymore.

My mom came to spend the day with me, and Reverend Bud stopped by. Dawn did not respond to either of them. Everyone, including the nurses, tried humoring her without any success.

In the evening when Dave came, I told him how she had been all day and that she wouldn't eat breakfast or lunch. He started to talk with her, but she just stared at him, too. When supper came, he tried to get her to eat. He used every approach, but nothing seemed to work. She kept saying no, which was more than I got out of her.

I could tell she was mad about having surgery again, so finally I said, "Dawn, you're mad, aren't you?"

She looked me right in the eye and sternly said, "Yes!"

I said, "Dawn, you have a right to be mad, but being mad and not eating will not get you out of this hospital."

Dave and I both talked to her until finally she decided to eat a little. I was wishing she would eat more, but I figured—now that she had expressed her anger—maybe she would put up a fight to get well.

That night, Dave wanted us both to go home. I wanted to stay, but getting some sleep in a bed sounded good. The nurses, too, through that again. Even the nurses noticed how tired I looked so they too encouraged me to leave. I was glad to get home, because I hadn't seen Lori and D. J. since Saturday. They had been staying with my mom and sister Willie. When we picked them up, D.J. was very glad to see me. Right away he wanted to know when I would be home to stay. I told him Dawn was better and that maybe in a few days she would be home.

Dawn's recovery went rather well the rest of the week. On Thursday she came out of ICU and was assigned a room with a talkative girl about her own age. She could also watch TV and have visitors. She had many visitors and received many get-well cards. People from the church sent cards, telling how they were praying for her to have a speedy recovery. I could see God's love being poured out through our church family and friends.

On Saturday, Dr. Gracias told us Dawn was well enough to go home on Sunday. We were all so excited that we cheered, even her roommate. We packed up all her belongings and took some home. We were excited the next morning when we picked her up. My sister Ann from Indiana and her family were staying at my mom's for the weekend. They all came over to our house to see Dawn. Dave decided to go fishing with my brother George while I stayed home with Dawn. He had been under so much tension that he wanted to relax. While Dawn slept, I went over to my mom's. All the kids were out in the yard playing ball. I joined my sister Barb and her husband Wally on the porch. Wally was coaching the kids from his wheelchair. Barb and I were involved in conversation, when all of a sudden we heard Lori scream, "Oh, my leg!" We ran off the porch and fond her on the ground. My two teenage nephews helped her to the porch. The leg was already swelled, and when we tried to move it, she cried, "Ouch!" Wally spoke up, saying, "I'll bet her leg is broken. I heard it crack when Rusty ran into her."Lori had covered home plate and when Rusty slid into home their legs hit". The rest of the family got upset over what had happen, each giving his or her version of what they'd seen. I went home and check on Dawn. I called Dave home from fishing. When he arrived we took Lori to the hospital emergency. On the way, I said over and over, "I don't believe this. We just left that hospital this morning, and now we're on our way back." Dave and I both kidded Lori about breaking her leg just so she could find out what it was like to go to the hospital emergency. Lori has a good sense of humor and didn't seem to mind but promptly said, "Mom, why would I want to ruin my summer vacation?" After spending a couple of hours in the emergency and X-ray rooms, the doctor came and told us her leg was broken. He said there was a little piece of bone that would have to be watched, because it might need a pin to keep it in place. She had to be in a cast from hip to toes for six weeks. He wanted her to stay in the hospital for a few days to monitor the swelling and have her on crutches before she came home. As Lori was wheeled up to her room, Dave and I walked along in disbelief. I said to Dave, "Do you think this is all just a bad dream?" He shook his head, saying, "I'm afraid this is reality." When we got to third-floor pediatrics, the nurse told us Lori would be put in Room 3025. I spoke up and said "I just took Dawn out of there this morning." When we got to the room, the empty bed for Lori was the one that Dawn had come out of that morning. The girl in the room was surprised when she saw us. We introduced her to Lori and told her about the accident.

On Monday, when I went to work, everyone wanted to know how it felt to have Dawn home. When I told them Lori was now in the hospital, they didn't believe me until I asked permission to take a long lunch so I could go see her. How was I going to divide my time between the two girls? I also wondered if Lori would expect me to be at the hospital with her as much as I was with Dawn.

I kept praying that the Lord would show me what to do, and when I got to the hospital, my answer came. I talked to Lori about the amount of time I should spend with her. She was very understanding, saying, "Mom, I know you have to be home with Dawn. You don't have to stay long at a time." I kissed her, saying, "You're such an understanding kid." I spent my time Monday through Thursday running back and forth from home, work, and hospital. By Thursday, when Lori came home, I was tired and wanted to drop. The doctor didn't want Lori to move around for at least a week after she came home, so I had to wait on her a lot. That first week of having Lori laid up helped me realize what a big help she had been.

The next few weeks were really rough. There was so much for me to do at night after work. Lori couldn't get around well, and

Dawn's recovery seemed slow. Dave helped me with the girls, but couldn't with my depression. Some days, I would do real well; on other days, I was in a daze from having so much on my mind.

My biggest problem was dealing with the changes in my life because of Dawn's illness. It seemed bad enough that I had to worry about the possibility of the cancer coming back, but now Dr. Gracias said she could have problems with her shunt. I couldn't help thinking that her shunt could plug up anytime, and Dr. Gracias would have to do major surgery to correct it. My life had changed, but Dawn's was even more affected. It was obvious that she wasn't growing. Her appetite was poor, causing her to stay thin. She'd had to change schools because of her learning disability, which was also hard to accept.

Some days I would run all the changes through my mind until my head ached so badly I'd have to lie down. Dave can cope with problems, which makes it very hard for him to understand why I worry so. Because we lacked understanding, there were lots of little arguments.

Hanging on to Faith

Soon after Dawn's latest surgery, a bomb fell on me. Dawn came to me and said, "Ma, my neck is sore." I checked her neck over thoroughly and discovered that it was very red in the area of her shunt. My heart sank. At first, I could hardly believe it and wondered how she could have gotten an infection so soon again. I said, "Oh, Dawn, I think your shunt is infected."

When I told Dawn about what was wrong with her neck, she started questioning me about whether or not she'd have to go to the hospital. She got upset at the idea of going back to the hospital yet again giving me a bland stare. I really didn't know, but I told her maybe she could be treated with antibiotics at home.

The next morning I called Dr. Gracias. When I told him what had happened, he said, "Meet me at the hospital right away." After hanging up, I felt scared. He sounded so concerned. I got Dawn ready immediately and met Dr. Gracias in the main lobby of the hospital. He took one look at her neck and said, "The shunt is infected again. She'll have to be admitted." Dawn looked away and would not talk to Dr Gracias or me. I could see she was upset by what was being said. A new doctor came on the scene. Dawn had to be seen by the hospital's infectious disease specialist, Dr. Cook. He was easy to talk to so I asked him lots of questions. The depressing news he told me was that Dawn had to be on an intravenous(IV) antibiotic for at least two weeks. I thought about Dawn's last hospital stay. Dr. Gracias had said then that if the infection didn't clear up, we'd know in thirty days. It had been just short of thirty days since the previous incidence of infection was discovered.

As Dr. Cook explained the dangers of the antibiotic he would be giving Dawn. I fought back tears. He was telling me the antibiotic was so thick that Dawn's little veins could collapse every few days. That meant that a new IV would have to be started each time. *How is she going to handle being poked for a new IV every few days?*

The day after Dawn was admitted, I met a family with a four-year-old boy who had had surgery for a similar brain tumor. They reminded me of Dave's and my situation during Dawn's first surgery. They were happy to hear Dawn had been in remission for three years but upset when I told them she was admitted because of an infected shunt. Their son also had a shunt.

As I shared our experiences with this family, I forgot my self-pity in order to lend a little comfort to them. I've found it is therapeutic to give comfort to someone in need. I'd already been through what they were just now experiencing.

On the third day of Dawn's first IV placement, her vein collapsed. When I got to her room, I saw her arm was swollen and red. The resident doctor reluctantly told me the IV would have to be placed in a new vein.

When the IV therapist came in and approached Dawn, she turned her head in distress. She knows when a person with a white coat, a plastic tote with tubes walks in they'll be probing her veins with a needle. This time was no exception. By the time the IV therapist found a good vein, Dawn was in tears, and I wanted to scream, *"Leave her alone!"* After she left, I tried to convince Dawn that the IV was better than having a shot every four hours. My talk didn't help much, because she lay in a disheartened mood the rest of the evening. I kept thinking about the possibility of her going through that process every two days. It's painful to see her so miserable. I started praying that God would comfort her and help her get through the next two weeks.

The next two weeks went better with Dawn than I expected. Our church family and friends were very supportive. Reverend Bud stopped by often with his upbeat personality. As Dawn's veins kept collapsing, it seemed that the IV people got used to her, because they got better at finding her veins.

The worst time was Labor Day weekend. There were few people around the hospital. The days were warm and sunny, the kind when you like to be outside. I wanted to take Dawn outside, but because of her IV pole, she had to stay in. It was hard to remain in that hot, gloomy room. I found myself just sitting, dwelling on Dawn's condition. We tried to make the weekend special by having Lori and D. J. come to the hospital and eat in the cafeteria with us. Even with that and having friends and family come to visit, I was glad when the weekend was over.

Finally the big day came. On September 12th, I loaded Dawn with all her flowers, gifts, and cards into the car. Dawn and I were two happy people, and we talked all the way home. This was the second time this summer that she had returned from the hospital. I prayed it would be the last. Dr. Gracias couldn't give us much hope that the infection would never come back. He could only say, "I hope we got it all this time." He explained that bacteria could hide in the brain anywhere, and until it became an infection, antibiotics wouldn't touch it.

The day after Dawn came home, I had an appointment with my gynecologist, Dr. Hydrick. When he finished my annual checkup, he said, "Your breasts are full of cysts. I would like you to see a surgeon about having them removed." I was surprised at his suggestion, though I'd been having pain because of them. My question to him was "why." "You are in a high-risk category for developing cancerous tumors, and with the cysts, it would be hard to tell a cyst from a tumor." He discussed it with me to some extent, and before I left, he made an appointment for me to see a plastic surgeon who specialized in silicone implants. When I went to the doctor, he gave me an exam and ordered X-rays. That meant another I couldn't stop thinking about it the rest of the day. I kept thinking how terrible it would be to have someone cut me all up. I felt so dispirited that I could hardly discuss the matter with Dave. He told me not to think about it until I got an opinion from a plastic surgeon. There were ten days between the time I saw Dr. Hydrick and the time I went to D. Corey, the plastic surgeon. I was very frightened during that time wait. I felt even worse when I left. Waiting was very hard.

With school approaching, I had to arrange for Dawn's education. I had talked to the school several times, but they kept telling me they were working on it. Finally the day came when they tested her and said they had a school in mind.

Dawn was feeling good but bored with staying home. When the call came that a Mrs. Smith, the special education representative, wanted us to visit Iroquois School in Grand Rapids, we were both elated.

Iroquois Middle School has a special education program called POHI, physically or health impaired. This program is conducted in a part of the school that is specially equipped for handicapped students. Because of Dawn's neurological impairment, she qualified. We were both impressed with the school. Her first question was, "When can I start?" With Dawn's answer we knew that she was ready for change. She came to terms with her difficulty in a normal school setting. She also realized her friends were well advanced over her and did not relate to her anymore. We could hardly wait to get home and tell the rest of the family about Dawn's new school.

Dawn started school right away. The first day she was so excited I could hardly keep her still long enough to eat breakfast. The minibus picked her up right in our driveway. Because of going to school twenty-one miles away, her days were long. She boarded the bus at 7:15 a.m. and didn't get home until 4:15 p.m.

She didn't like having to give up her friends at school in Wayland, but it wasn't long before she made new ones at Iroquois. The only disadvantage was that because of getting home so late, she couldn't call or see her new friends after school.

Dawn made a good adjustment to Iroquois Middle School. It was a relief to have her school situation resolved.

The big day came for Lori to have her walking cast taken off on November 1st. She was *very* happy, because walking in a cast had cramped her style. She was in the tenth grade in high school, with lots of activities that couldn't be done with a cast on. When the cast came off, she said, "I feel like a free person again!" I kept thinking of how wonderful it would be if Dawn's healing could be like that. Dawn would like so much to be a free person, too.

A few days after taking Lori to the doctor, I had to go see Dr. Corey again. I was pleasantly surprised when he told me he didn't want to do surgery on my breasts right now. He thought the silicone implant would be too risky at this time. He explained how the cysts were so involved in the nerve tissue that an implant might not be possible. He also said he didn't think the risk of getting cancer at this time was any higher than the risk of the surgery. When I left Dr. Corey's office, I had mixed feelings—happy not to be facing surgery but worried about the other risks.

Things went along pretty well for a while, until a parent-teacher conference in late November. Dawn hadn't talked much about school the past few weeks so I assumed everything was going okay. She was happy just to be in school again. When I went for the conference, several teachers said Dawn was doing poorly and that she wasn't able to do eighth grade math and social studies. After I got over the hurt of what they were saying, I asked why they expected her to be able to do the work at her grade level knowing she had serious neurological damage.

After talking to Dawn's teachers at length, we decided to have her tested to determine her learning level. I remembered how well she had done before. She'd had to give up so much, and I resented that this ability was being taken away from her.

When all the tests were done, it was clear that Dawn's ability was at a sixth- grade level. They said she hadn't lost any of the knowledge she'd gained up until then but seemed to be having trouble retaining new material. I was unhappy to hear all this, even though I had suspected it. Previously, Dawn had shown the most scholastic ability of our three kids. Now, they were telling me that it would be difficult for her.

I pondered this news for quite a while. My hopes and dreams for Dawn seemed to be losing ground.

I wondered how she'd react to this news. I didn't want to tell her she would have to study material that she'd already had.

The teachers said they would have her review old material and slowly try to add to it, a little at a time, depending on her progress.

When I approached Dawn about her schoolwork, she became very defensive, saying she'd have to work harder. I was pleased about her spirit but worried about going through the same stress we went through the prior two years. I didn't want to see her come home every night and worry about getting a lot of homework done.

The kids were busy all fall with school and church activities. I was involved in church work, too. Reverend Bud had recruited me as Sunday School Superintendent a few years ago, and each year I seemed to have more responsibilities. I liked working with Sunday school; it made me feel I could do something important as one of God's servants. I had never really done a whole lot for God, so I wanted to do a good job as superintendent.

Even though I stayed active with church, home, and work activities, I still had time to worry about Dawn and be cross because of my arthritis pain. Dave never knew what to expect from me when I came home at night. Some days the pain was so bad in my leg and back that I was very hard to live with.

One day, I finally got some insight as to handling my problem. My mother and I went to an arthritis lecture given by a top rheumatologist at Butterworth Hospital. After the doctor talked, several people talked about their arthritis. They told about the problem they had with their families understanding the pain they lived with. As I sat there listening, I thought how their problems were similar to mine.

At the end of the lecture, the doctor asked for questions. I was encouraged, after I explained to the doctor my job situation and the pain I suffered, that he didn't say I should quit. He suggested that I have a little footstool in front of my cash register to rest my leg on. He said I should shift my weight around by resting each leg at different times.

My whole attitude changed after that night. I felt as though someone really understood me and my pain. Dave was really happy to see the change and quickly built the little stool I *needed* for work. I was teased about my stool, which several people referred to as a bird house, but I found it to be so helpful that I didn't care. By lifting my leg a short distance off the floor, it took a lot of pressure off my back and leg at the same time.

When the new year came, Dave and I again found ourselves looking forward to it with hope. I was finally getting some relief from pain, and Dawn was getting along in school. I continued to pray that I'd be able to handle each problem that came along and that this would be a good year.

I entered 1979 with great expectations, but it wasn't long before hope was crushed again. Off and on through the first few months, Dawn would complain of headaches and sometimes dizziness. I tried not to worry, but she was always on my mind. Every time she complained, I wondered if her shunt was plugging up or the cancer was returning.

My only outlet was the monthly cancer meetings. I always knew that the parents there would listen to my fear and understand. I didn't dare share my fears with Dave, because he already thought I worried too much. Besides the parents at the cancer meetings, we often had an interesting speaker who would talk on related subjects. I never left a meeting without feeling better than when I went. Some parents had more problems than I did, so that would make me stop and think that it could be worse.

I tried to develop different ways to deal with my stress. Besides the cancer meetings, I had the opportunity to take a short course in stress management. I found it very helpful. It didn't take away my stress, but at least I understood how to handle it a little better.

When spring approached, Dave and I decided to take the kids on a trip during their spring break. After discussing it as a family, we decided to go to the Smoky Mountains. We had a lot of fun planning the trip, even forgetting about Dawn's shunt for a while.

On March 30th, we packed up the camper and took off toward Ohio and Tennessee.

During our first night in Ohio, Dawn became very sick. She kept saying she couldn't breathe. I was awake most of the night with her because she was so disoriented. As usual, 1 kept worrying about her shunt. Dave tried to reassure me that it was just her stuffy nose and that she'd be okay.

We went to the store and bought some decongestive tablets. All day I worried about whether we should go on with our trip. I didn't like taking her so far away from Dr. Gracias. I kept thinking, *If it is her shunt, what will we do so far away from home?* That was a real scary thought. Every time I'd talk to Dave, he'd say, "She'll be all right. Don't worry."

I didn't want to ruin the trip for everyone, so after we visited my cousins for a couple of days, we went on. I prayed and continued to give Dawn the pills, which eventually cleared up her stuffiness.

The time we spent going through the mountains was spiritually rewarding. We spent a lot of time just looking at the view. There was *much* peace there. We all kept talking about how, if anyone doubted there was a God, that person should come to these mountains. No one other than God could create such majesty. I came out of the mountains feeling closer to God and with a renewed belief that He was really with us.

On our way home, we stopped in Kentucky at the home of our friends, Karen and Bill. They were so filled with God's love that they were a joy to be around. While we were at their home, they gave us a tour of the seminary, Shaker Town, and many other interesting sights. We concluded the weekend by attending their large church. The average attendance on Sunday is a thousand people. We were all much impressed with the Sunday school and with the worship service. We felt spiritually filled when we came away. It was a great way to finish a great family vacation. We were thankful that Dawn had done so well. She enjoyed herself as much as the rest of us.

Soon after we got back from vacation, it was Lori's and Dawn's birthdays. Lori surprised me by saying she didn't want to celebrate with Dawn this year, because she was going to be sixteen and wanted to have a party by herself. At first I was hurt. I kept thinking that one of these days she might not have a sister to celebrate with. How could she want to start then?

After discussions with both girls, they decided that Lori would celebrate on April 25th, the day of their birthday, and Dawn would celebrate on the 27th with a slumber party. Dawn's slumber party went well, but it was very obvious that she was way behind her friends, both in growth and maturity. I was pleased that her friends made her feel a part of them, even though she had been away from most of them over a year. When Dawn's birthday celebration was over, I prayed, "Lord, let her have another birthday next year."

Dawn's shunt continued to be troublesome. She'd often complain about headaches and dizziness again. During that time, Reverend Bud helped me to realize that God could understand our deepest feelings and needs. If there is something we don't want to share with another person, we can always entrust it to God.

In May, we learned Reverend Bud would be leaving for another church. We would get a new pastor by the name of

Reverend Barker. At first I was crushed. I thought, *How am I going to share my feelings with a new pastor who won't know me?* It was scary at first, but because Reverend Barker and his family were such spirit-filled people, it didn't take long to get acquainted.

———————•———————

When summer came, I again found Dawn spending a lot of time by herself. She didn't have a lot in common with her friends, so they didn't come over. Every time I saw her sitting by herself, looking lonely, I cried inside. I tried to spend some time with her by going on bike rides. We had a good time riding together.

All three kids went to church camp, with Dawn also going to the cancer camp. She loved going to camp but always came home tired. After spending a week at camp, she'd sleep for days afterward. The cancer camp she went to was called Special Days. It was well staffed with a doctor, nurses, and many volunteers. I didn't have to worry about her. With all the kids there having had cancer at one time in their lives, she was around kids she could relate well to.

After coming home from a camping trip as a family, we heard the tragic news about our close friends' daughter. I went into a state of shock when the call came. Al and Herta's daughter, Debbie, was killed in an auto accident. When we went to the funeral home that night, I was at a loss for words. I didn't know how to console these close friends. Debbie, at twenty-three years of age, was right in the prime of life. How could God let such a thing happen?

The day of Debbie's funeral, I found the comfort I needed. The pastor who talked at her funeral was fantastic. He had such comforting words to say. He stressed that even though we grieve, Debbie was happy with Jesus. She was a Christian, and now, because of that, she entered a new life with Him. Everything he said that day made me feel happy for Debbie, but what about the family and friends she left behind? How do they cope without her presence? My mind kept going over the fact that someday I might have to suffer the pain my friends did. The idea of giving up Dawn, even to a better life, seemed like too much to bear.

As summer was coming to a close, Dave and I started talking about taking a trip to Hawaii in January. I'd been writing to a pen pal there for twenty-one years, and I was eager to meet her. For fifteen years, Dave and I had been saving toward the trip, but things kept getting in the way. We were always using our money for something else. Dave decided that we again had enough money to go and that waiting any longer didn't make much sense. He felt we both needed to get away, and I agreed. The day we went to the travel bureau and made our plans was the most exciting day for us in years. We were like newlyweds when we came away with our travel plans in hand. All the way home, we talked about the dream trip come true and how exciting it would be to meet my pen pal(Patty) after all these years of writing to her. I could hardly wait to get home and write her about our plans.

Things seemed to go along pretty well until October, when Dawn started acting strangely again. She wet the bed a lot and was sometimes very hyper. I didn't know what to think. When things didn't get any better, I took her in to see Dr. Taylor.

Dr. Taylor checked Dawn's shunt and said it was very sluggish. Right away, he advised me to take her to Dr. Gracias. I called Dr. Gracias and found that he wanted a CAT scan to be done. It was done the next day. It turned out negative, which meant there was not enough pressure on the brain to make a change of the shunt necessary. If the scan showed a lot of pressure, it would mean the shunt was plugged somewhere.

I was relieved that the scan was negative, but this meant her problems came from some other source.

Two weeks after Dawn had the scan, she became disoriented. I kept her home from school because she acted so strangely. She didn't sleep at night and kept getting into things like a two-year-old child. This was strange behavior for her.

On October 27th, she wet and had a bowel movement in her bed. She got upset with me when I asked her about it. She had the bed torn apart, trying to cover up her mess.

When the same thing happened again the next night, I called Dr. Gracias. He said, "Bring her to the hospital tomorrow, and we'll admit her for tests."

"Oh no," I said to myself, "here we go again." The idea of putting her in the hospital again for tests sounded terrible. How was I going to tell her?

There was my job to consider, too. If Dawn was going to have tests, I wanted to be there with her. My store had changed owners in May. Art Haan, the former owner, had gotten to know about my problem with Dawn. Now I'd be dealing with new owners and a new work schedule. My old hours were 8:00 a.m. to 5:00 p.m. Now they varied daily. The store manager and head cashier were still the same people, so I thought maybe they would understand my need to be with Dawn. Art Haan had treated all of his employees as friends. Whenever we had a problem, we could go to him, and he'd listen. I wondered what it would be like with Robert Woodrick, the new owner. He was the President of D& W Food Centers, with hundreds of employees. I wondered what effect my absence from work would have on my job.

I had always worked for a small family-operated business, so the last few months working for D& W was different. The benefits were great, but the relaxed atmosphere that came from knowing the owner was missing. It was also harder to deal with customer complaints because there were so many people to go through. I was thankful this new problem with Dawn hadn't come up when the store was going through the transitional period. I called the store the next day letting them know I would not be in. The head cashier seemed to understand when I told her why I would not be in. She went on to say, "Just keep in touch."

I took Dawn to the hospital by myself the next day. It was a lonely ride into Grand Rapids. Dawn didn't say much, and I knew why. Neither one of us wanted to spend time there.

She was put in a private room at the end of the isolation wing. Dawn and I both liked being around people, so neither of us liked the room. As soon as the nurse came in, I asked, "Why is Dawn here in a private room?"

She said, "Because it's the room her doctor wanted."

I could not figure out why he wanted her in a private room. He knew Dawn liked being with other kids. I also wondered if Dave's insurance would pay for it.

When Dr. Gracias came in to see Dawn, I asked him about the room. He explained that he wanted to keep her there until he knew whether she had an infected shunt. I asked if she could be moved as soon as he knew, and he said, "yes." I knew Dawn would not want to be by herself so wanted her where she would at least have a roommate.

The first day went by slowly. The only test performed was a CAT scan, and we found out that was negative and didn't tell them anything new. I knew now that finding her problem would be difficult.

Dawn was restless the second day. She asked me questions about her condition and how long she'd have to be there. I didn't have any comforting answers.

The EEG test she had that day didn't tell them anything either, and I was discouraged at the results. Every negative test she had only meant more tests.

Dawn kept putting her arms around me and crying. I tried to find out why she was crying, but she just kept shaking her head. I put her on my lap and held her close. She finally blurted out, "I don't want any more tests." Because of the tests over the last two days with no answers we both knew there would be more.

Mothers are supposed to protect and comfort their children, and I couldn't seem to do either for her. I cried with her and said, "I can't make your problems go away, but I'll stay with you as much as I can." After we had a good cry and I hugged her a lot, she got back into bed for a nap.

Reverend Barker came up that evening to see her. I shared Dawn's fears with him. He led us in prayer; that really helped. I needed that reasureance to help me get through me that God was going to help her get through this ordeal.

Even before I left for the night, Dawn had wet the bed. I stayed for a while and helped the nurses get her cleaned up. As I was helping one of them with Dawn's nightgown, I noticed a discolored spot on her head. I rubbed my hand on it and found that it felt soft. The nurse looked at it and said she'd report it to the resident doctor on duty.

When Dr. Gracias came by the next day, he said he wasn't sure what test to do next. He looked at the spot on Dawn's head and said it could be a blood clot. He was going to talk to some other doctors for another opinion. It's hard to realize doctors can't solve some medical problems easily. I always felt they knew what to do right away, but then I'd never had to deal with serious ailments.

Dawn was in a cheerful mood that night, and I decided to go to work Thursday morning. I was so upset after the phone call that I couldn't work. Business had slowed down a little, so the person in charge let me leave. Then I wondered if that was a mistake. My mind kept drifting off to the hospital, which caused me to make silly mistakes. One customer said to me, "Are you okay? You don't look too cheerful." I briefly explained to her, and she was very understanding. Each time the phone rang, I feared my name would be called. Just before 2:00 p.m.. that fear became a reality. Dr. Gracias called to tell me he had decided to do surgery the next day. He said he'd give me the details when I got to the hospital. I couldn't get to the hospital fast enough. I kept wondering what Dr. Gracias had found that made him decide on surgery.

I found Dawn in good spirits when I got there. She didn't know about the surgery, and I dreaded telling her. Dr. Gracias arrived soon after Dave and outlined the surgery to the three of us. He had to take care of the blood clot and to check the valve on the shunt. Dawn took it better than I thought she would, but then Dr. Gracias had a caring way of explaining things. She was showing great trust in him. Dave and I shared that trust. Reverend Barker and some friends and relatives must have sensed our need for company, because quite a few came up that night. It really helped to keep our minds off the surgery. Before Reverend Barker left, he prayed a very comforting prayer. It helped us to go home with some peace of mind.

We went to the hospital early the next morning to see Dawn before she went for surgery. We found her in good spirits. Reverend Barker arrived soon after Dawn was given her pre-op shot. He led us in prayer, as we all sat nervously waited for the surgical escort service to arrive.

At 9:00 a.m., Dawn was wheeled off to surgery, and I found myself sitting in the surgical waiting room for the fourth time. I tried to make conversation with Reverend Barker and Dave, but my mind kept drifting off. Reverend Barker had brought a devotional guidebook, which I read for a time. The devotions were helpful, but my concentration was way off.

The room was filled with families waiting for news of loved ones. I couldn't help wondering how many people in the room had been there before. I never dreamed four years ago that I would be back there so many times.

At 11:20 a.m., Dr. Gracias came in with a positive look. His first words in response to my wide eyes/clenched hands were, "Dawn is going to be fine. I put a new pump on the shunt and removed a blood clot from the top of her skull."

I breathed a sigh of relief.

Reverend Barker led us in a prayer of thanksgiving for God being with Dawn and the doctor during surgery. Dave and I hugged each other, as a sign that we had once again gotten through another rough time.

In the afternoon, as we sat by Dawn's bed waiting for her to wake up, I prayed for her to have a full recovery. I wanted God to perform one of His miracle healings. I'd heard much about miracle healings but never met anyone who had received one. In my prayer I said, "God, if you give Dawn a complete healing, I'll see that Your name is fully praised." I didn't want her going through life struggling just to survive. Dawn slept most of the day, only waking up to look around to see if we were there. Toward 7:00 p.m., I couldn't make up my mind if we should leave or not. Lori was going to be performing with the band as a flag girl and was eager for us to see the band perform. I wanted to see Lori but couldn't pull myself away from Dawn. I was afraid that she would wake up and want me. Dave sensed my indecision and said, "It's about time we leave. We told Lori we'd be back in time to see the band." I agreed and reluctantly said good-bye to Dawn.

I knew that Dawn was in good hands, but I always liked to be with her when she was in ICU. She had never liked being in there and had always done better if I was there. Dawn seemed to understand what I was saying when I explained why we were leaving. Her spirits were good, and she was able to give us a big hug and kiss. We made it back to Wayland just as the band was marching onto the field. I was filled with pride when I spotted Lori with the flag corps. Its performance was great, and I was glad we decided to go and see it. As soon as we started toward home, my mind went back to the hospital. It was hard to know how to divide my time. I knew Lori and D. J. had a right to some of it. With a child in the hospital, the ones at home usually get left out for a while.

I called the hospital at 7:00 a.m. Saturday morning to see how Dawn went through the night. The nurse in charge said she was doing fine. I decided to fix breakfast and eat with Dave and the kids before I left. I wasn't nervous now that I had called the hospital. While we were eating breakfast, Lori mentioned how happy she was that Dave and I had seen her perform. I gave her a big hug, saying, "Lori, I was very proud of you!" D.J. spoke up and said, "Ma, how long are you going to be at the hospital today?" I said, "I'll be back early if Dawn does well all day." I knew he had a right to want me home, and I hated going away with the pressure of his wanting me to stay.

———•———

When I arrived at the ICU wing Saturday morning, I found a very busy nursing staff. Dawn was in a four-bed room that had received two more patients—two fussy toddlers—during the night. I went to Dawn to see if she was awake. I kissed her but didn't receive a response. I decided she was sleeping so I settled down in an easy chair to wait. I noticed the other children in the room. I didn't know what was wrong with them but could tell one of them must have had an accident of some kind. There were no other parents there yet, and one small boy kept crying for his mother.

As I sat there listening to the boy crying and the other activities in the room.

I wondered how Dawn was accepting being in ICU again. In the past, she never responded very well. "Please, dear Lord," I prayed, "helps her get through the ordeal of being here again."

A nurse came and took Dawn's vital readings and reported that her blood pressure was low. I wondered what that meant. Soon after the nurse left, Dawn started moving her legs uncontrollably. I asked the nurse to come back with the ring of the call bell. I was in a panic about what was happening. I held her legs with hopes she would not go off the bed. By the time she returned, Dawn's legs were off the bed. I helped the nurse straighten out her legs. The nurse said, "Dawn appears to be having some kind of spasm."

That was only the beginning of a nightmare. During the day her condition continued to worsen. Her blood pressure stayed down and the spasms continued. I didn't get to talk to her. I kept trying to get a response but none was forthcoming. She seemed to be unconscious cause her eyes were shut and she did not respond to my calls out to her.

Doctors kept coming in to see her, but left the room to talk. I wondered what was going on but was afraid to ask. Their faces told me that they were as worried as I was. They had such concerned looks with frowns with out making eye contact with me.

Dr. Gracias had to be out of town the day after surgery, so I knew he wasn't around. The nurse came in and said Dr. John would be up soon to examine Dawn. Dr. John was covering for Dr. Gracias this weekend, and I knew he wouldn't have been in unless it was urgent.

Visitors kept coming all afternoon. It was hard for me to visit with them, because they couldn't enter Dawn's room, and I didn't want to leave. I expressed to them my concern for the way she was acting. They could see by my tears and tissue in had that I was so upset. Everyone tried to comfort me, but the anxiety kept building. By the time Dave arrived around 4:00 p.m., I was a wreck. I ran to him and cried out, "Dawn isn't doing very well." He had me sit down and explained what had transpired.

While we were talking, Dr. John came and examined Dawn. I watched his facial expressions. With the frown and not making eyecontact I knew he too was worried. When he was through, he said, "This is serious. I'm not sure what is going on, but we'd better get a CAT scan done right away. There is a possibility that the shunt might be malfunctioning again and could be causing pressure on the brain."

If the shunt was plugged, it would mean more surgery. How could Dawn's body stand having another operation so soon. It had only been two days since the last one. Dr. John went over all the possibilities then left to order a scan.

I fell into Dave's arms and cried. I was scared. So many scary thoughts went through my mind that I developed a terrible headache. I thought about what had happened between the time I left her the night before and now. I was angry at myself for leaving her. What if she did not wake up? I started praying earnestly, "Please, dear God, don't let anything worse happen to her."

It wasn't long until the ambulance came and took Dawn for her scan. I wanted to go, but they asked us to wait. Her nurse went with them. As they left, she said, "Try not to worry. We'll find out what's wrong." I couldn't get over the way Dawn looked. Her face was very pale. When they moved her, I noted that her body was limp. *What if she doesn't come back alive?*

Living with Fear

Dave and I were sitting in the lobby when my cousins, Tom and Shirley, got off the elevator. I was glad to see them and quickly explained what was happening. Shirley had lost her first husband to a brain disorder, so I knew she'd understand my fear.

It seemed like we sat for hours, waiting. Finally, Dave and I were called to ICU where Dr. John waited to tell us of the results.

The scan showed increased cranial pressure. "I'm going into her body and check the pump on the shunt," he said. He talked of the dangers of surgery but said it was her only chance. I felt sick with fear feeling my heart pump so fast I wanted to scream.

My fears mounted as we walked to the surgical waiting room—the second time in two days for Dave and me. I wondered how many more times I would be there.

When Dr. John walked through the door, I knew by the look on his pale sad face that the news wasn't good. I jumped up, and the others stood anxiously. Dr. John said, "Please sit down and I'll try to explain. I changed the pump on the shunt, but I'm not sure I helped her any." He went on to say that everything seemed to check out okay. Then the bad news fell like an axe. He said, "I think the cancer is seeding. It could be so small that it can't be picked up by the CAT scan." I couldn't believe what I was hearing.

He said he had seen something in the X-ray that did not look normal. He said it with such a uncaring business like tone of voice.

By the time Dr. John finished talking and left, I hated him. I screamed to Dave, "What right does Dr. John have saying the cancer is seeding?" I walked the floor while pulling on my hair towards my face.

Word of Dawn's surgery had reached home, so my sister Willie, and her husband Louie, and Reverend Barker came to the hospital at once. We were glad to see them, but when they came, I was too angry to say much. I heard Dave telling them about the surgery and what Dr. John had said. I jumped into the conversation and said, "There is no evidence of cancer seedings." I did not believe what the doctor said so was not willing to listen to anynore cancer talk. I could tell by there sad looks at me that they believed the doctor. I didn't want everyone saying Dawn had cancer again. The word sounded fatal.

Reverend Barker got us all in a circle for prayer. My tears and anger had taken over, leaving me unable to appreciate what was being said. The others tried to offer words of comfort, but I didn't feel they could understand how I was feeling. I did listen to my cousin Shirley some. Having lost her first husband, I figured she knew something of my anguish.

Dawn's pediatrician, Dr. Taylor, came by to see how we were doing. I tried to listen to what he had to say but didn't like what he said either. He said, "We knew there was a possibility of this happening, didn't we?" I cried even harder, holding my face in my hands, unwilling to look at anyone. I did not want to see ther look of defeat.

Those around thought they could comfort me by saying, "Dawn has lived four years longer than they thought she would." I shook my head in agreement with them. But on the inside, I hated them for using such words to try to comfort me. Even Dave tried to comfort me by saying that we had some good times with Dawn and should appreciate them.

When Dave and I went back to ICU, I sat looking at Dawn and thinking about all she had been through. I kept saying to her, "Dawn, you can't give up now. You've got to fight." I held her hand while I talked to her and prayed. The nurse that was taking care of her tried to be of help, but I still wanted to be left alone. I knew by the look on her face and from what she said that she, too, thought Dawn had cancer again. There was no comfort in visiting with anyone who believed that.

Throughout the entire night, I kept my hand in hers the whole time, feeling that she was in one of her depressions from the surgery and wasn't fighting. If I could convince her to fight, God would help her to get well. I kept pleading by saying, "Dawn, please fight. I need you and love you very much. Please, Dawn, if you fight, God will help you get better."

It was difficult to believe that God might take her away, even though I knew parents who had lost children. Did I have any right to think Dawn wouldn't die because I was special? No, I thought Dawn was special. I believed God wanted her to live so she could be a witness to His love and healing. She had come this far, surely He wanted her to keep going.

When Dave walked into the room at 7:00 a.m. the next morning, my eyes were red and tired from crying. He must have thought I looked terrible, because he put his arms around me and said, "Will you please leave"? Between the nurse and Dave, I felt forced to go lie down.

After being on the couch less than an hour, I came back into the room, not able to stand being away from her. I needed to know what was going on in case there was a change. Dave didn't like it that I came back so soon, but I guess he realized he couldn't keep me away. The nurse brought us some coffee and asked us to eat the food off Dawn's tray. She said, "You two have to keep up your strength, or you won't be much help to Dawn." It was obvious that she was right, but I didn't have an appetite.

Mrs. Miller, the head nurse who had taken care of Dawn in the past, walked in and asked how I thought Dawn was. I told her I thought she was depressed from surgery and from being in ICU with crying babies. She said, "Let's move Dawn into a room across the hall by herself. There she won't hear the babies so much."

That sounded like a good idea. I talked to Dawn as if she were awake and told her about the move. When the change was made, I continued to tell her about the nice view from the room and how bright and sunny the day was. I turned on the radio I brought from home in the hope that she'd feel more at home.

Mrs. Miller also talked to her in a positive way by saying, "Dawn, you get better, and we won't have you here with us very long. We'll let you go on the main floor with the other teenagers."

As the day went on, there wasn't much change. Dawn remained unresponsive all day. My mom and dad, people from the church, and family and friends came throughout the day. It appeared that God was surrounding Dave and me with His love by using these people. Even though things looked bad, I felt God's presence through them.

When it got to be late at night and Dawn still hadn't responded, I told Dave I was going to stay overnight again. He was not happy but understood my need to stay. He decided to go home and sleep so he could work Monday. Before leaving, he gave me a kiss and warm embrace, saying, "Try to sleep, honey. She'll be okay." I needed to hear him say she'd be all right, because I thought maybe he believed what Dr. John had said.

I settled in an easy chair beside Dawn's bed and continued to hold her hand and talk to her. The nurses were very good to me. They offered me coffee while giving encouraging words. Two of the nurses that took care of Dawn had taken care of her before, so we'd sit and talk about some of her past stays at the hospital.

A couple of times during the night, Dawn opened her eyes. I felt so encouraged by this, and so did the nurses. I kept praying and talking, so I didn't sleep much. Just before morning, Dawn started moving a little, as if she was restless. I said, "Dawn, are you cold?" I was so excited when I heard her say yes and then roll over on her side. I put another blanket on her and called the nurse. She, too, got excited. By the time Dave came at six, I was jumping up and down. When I told him what had happened, he bent down saying, "Dawn, are you going to wake up for Dad today?" By the time the doctors started coming by to check her, she was wide awake. She wouldn't say anything, but her shining eyes responded to my voice. I was so excited I wanted to shout praises to God from the rooftop. I walked about the room singing shouts of joy and hugged the two nurses that walked in.

The doctors who came in to check her all agreed that she was much improved. I told them that I felt her biggest problem was depression and that she hadn't been fighting. I could tell they didn't quite go along with my theory, but they didn't have any better explanation for her sudden progress.

By lunchtime, Dawn was responding so well that her nurse, Mary, and I decided to get her up in a chair. She was really cooperative but didn't say anything. She just gave me a sad look as if to say ok I will do this. Just seeing her sitting in a chair after her unresponsiveness for so long made me very happy and excited. I kept talking to her, telling her how great she looked. When I asked, "Dawn, are you going to fight hard so God can help you get well?" she nodded her head. I grabbed her and gave her a big hug and kiss with tears of happiness and said, "Oh, thank you, God, for making my daughter fight again." I was sure, with God's help, she'd get well once again. I couldn't believe there was cancer seeding, as Dr. John suggested.

As Dr. Gracias and I stood talking about what went on with Dawn while he was gone, another doctor joined us. Dr. Gracias asked the resident doctor if he agreed with Dr. John's diagnosis. He said he did and expressed the need for more tests. I spoke up saying, "Can you do anything if you do find out you are right?"

They sadly said, "No."

"Well then, don't do any more tests on her, not even blood tests," was my desperate response. I wanted them to know by my voice that she needed to be left along for now.

Before they left, the doctors agreed they wouldn't do any more tests. They'd just wait and see how she responded. I felt relieved. I figured if Dawn was coming out of a depression, she'd do better not being poked with more needles.

She kept improving to the point that by Tuesday at 5:00 p.m. the doctors let her move from ICU into Pediatrics Main. During the day, she had sat up, gone for a walk with me, and had eaten some of her meals. When we moved her into a room with a roommate and TV, she smiled. It appeared likely at this point that her past problem was depression. Her new roommate's name was Sara. She had broken bones from a car accident. Sara had been in the hospital three weeks and had four or more to go. I felt Sara would be good therapy for Dawn because of Sara's apparent long stay. "I'm going to work now; I'll see you tonight. You get better and we'll get you out of here soon."

All morning, Dawn showed more and more signs of improvement. being confined to bed. In the past, She had always been roommates with girls who could get up, move around, and go home before she was able to. Maybe this time she would be first.

Dawn was so much improved by Wednesday night that I decided to go back to work Thursday. My boss was so good about letting me off from work that I felt I should go when I could. Although nervous, I made it through most of the day. As soon as business slowed down, they let me leave early in order to get to the hospital. I was thankful that D& W was that understanding about my need to be with Dawn.

By the weekend, Dawn was so improved that she wanted to go home. I talked to Dr. Gracias about it. He said, "I'll let Dawn go home as soon as she is eating better and walking more." Dawn had never eaten well while she was in the hospital, so I had to keep encouraging her. He also said he wanted to do another CAT scan before she left.

The next week things stayed about the same. I spent my time working and then going to the hospital, being at home only to sleep. Not being able to see much of D.J. and Lori bothered me. I kept praying that Dawn would improve enough that she could go home. My nerves were wearing down from the daily stress. Our family and friends continued coming to the hospital to visit. Everyone tried to encourage Dawn to eat, so she'd gain her strength back. Cards kept pouring in until we had the wallboard filled. So many prayers were being said in her behalf I felt God's love surrounding us. On Thursday of the next week, another CAT scan was done. While waiting for the results I sat in the lobby visiting with my friend, Maryann, I saw Dr. John go into ICU, and I said to Maryann, "There goes Dr. John." Responding to my nervousness, she said, "Go ask him about the CAT scan." I admitted to her that I was a little bit afraid of what the results might be. She then said, "It's better you find out than to just guess." When Dr. John came out, he said, "The scan looks very good. I didn't think I had helped her, but I guess I did. The ventricles are very small, indicating the shunt is working well again. We can't be sure about the cancer seedings, but she seems to be doing very well, and that's something."

I was so happy about the scan that I didn't care what he thought about cancer seedings. I decided to try really hard not to think about it. Dawn was better, and I was going to be taking her home. That was more hope than I had the week before.

On Saturday, two weeks after she lay almost lifeless, Dawn came home. Dr. Gracias was so happy about the scan that he said, "She's going to grow up to be a young lady yet." I could tell he shared my joy and happiness over her progress. He wasn't too happy about her sixty-nine-pound weight, though, and ordered her to eat more. Dr. Taylor had tested her thyroid, finding it to be very low. She had been on thyroid pills while in the hospital. When she came home she was on Dilantin to prevent seizures and thyroid problems. I was happy to have her home, but there was some fear in my heart of what her future might be. I kept wordering about her future with having so many health issues. She had been such a active child that seeing her so far behind her age group was hard. Also living with the fact that we may have to give her up to God. She got up feeling good on Sunday morning. She even wanted to get dressed. As she stood waiting for me to comb her hair(wig), she said, "Mom, what was I in the hospital for this time?" I was very surprised but tried not to let it show as I explained to her what had happened. This turned out to be one of many times I saw that her memory wasn't good.

The fear I had for Dawn's future made me realize I'd have to lean more on God if I was going to handle upcoming problems. The doctors couldn't give me any assurance that things would go well for her. I felt that she was brought home on faith that God would help us cope.

Dawn's recovery seemed to go slowly after she came home. Her appetite was poor. She stumbled around a lot and complained of headaches often. There was great concern for her despite much prayer. I continued to work, leaving her with my mom during the day, never sure what to expect when I came home at night. Dave and I talked over Dawn's problems, trying to decide what to do. I didn't want to call her doctor for fear he'd feel the need to run tests and wasn't sure which doctor should be called. Dr. Gracias would always ask me if I'd talked with Dr. Taylor. Dr. Taylor always wanted to know if I'd consulted Dr. Gracias. Dave and I ended up with the decision—on our own—to cut down on her Dilantin. She was only taking 200 mg. before her recent surgery. Because of the problems after her last two operations, the doctors decided to up the dosage to 300 mg. Dave felt very strongly that she was taking too much Dilantin. I decided to go along with him and tell Dr. Gracias about our decision when we took her in.

I watched Dawn even closer after we decreased the Dilantin but didn't see much change. She still walked terribly and became restless at night. We wondered whether her restlessness was something new or was because of decreasing the drug.

One evening we had been up to my sister's house. As we were coming out the back door, Dawn took a hard fall. She cried, saying, "Mom, my head hurts!" I worried about her all night, blaming myself for her fall. She wanted to be independent, so it was hard to know how much help we should give her.

I noticed that she asked me a lot of the same questions—over and over. If I said, "Dawn, you've already asked me that," she'd say she didn't remember. I realized now that memory was not good and she did not know it because she did not get upset at me telling her that. I wondered if this problem would continue and how it would affect her schoolwork when she went back.

I was constantly uptight about Dawn's slow progress but felt a little encouraged when she asked to go back to school. It appeared that she wouldn't be able to keep up with school but with her begging and Dave's saying I worried too much, it was decided that she should try.

Her first day back, on December 3rd, went well. She came home happy but very tired and slept most of the evening. She was too sleepy to eat much supper. I asked her if she thought school was going to be too hard. Her answer was, "Mom, don't worry. I'll be okay." I gave her a hug, feeling so proud of her strong spirit. The next day, on Tuesday, Dawn had to see Dr. Gracias for her checkup. After he examined her, his comment was, "She sure seems to be doing well." I proceeded to tell him about the problems we saw and how I couldn't stop thinking about Dr. John's idea of her having cancer seedings. He said very strongly, shaking his head, "Forget about that! Put that out of your mind completely. I don't feel that is happening to her." This was a substantial relief to us.

I also discussed my fear about continuing with the plans Dave and I had of going to Hawaii. He right away said, "Go, you need that vacation. I'll take care of Dawn for you." I thanked him for his offer and said, "She'll be staying with my mother." He was very much in agreement with that idea and said he'd help her with any problems that might come up. After telling him about decreasing Dawn's Dilantin pills, he expressed disagreement with our doing it without consulting him or Dr. Taylor. However, he said it was okay to keep the dosage down to see how she did. By the time we finished discussing Dawn's problems and Dave's and my trip, I felt differently about everything. He seemed to have a way of reassuring me that everything would be all right. The way Dawn would light up when he talked, you could tell she had a lot of confidence in him. As we were leaving, Dr. Gracias walked out into the waiting room to talk with Mom. He gave her all kinds of instructions on what to do while we were gone. Before he finished, he said, "Grandma, if Dawn needs me, call and ask for me, saying you're a friend." I felt really good as we left his office that day. It was such a great feeling to know he cared enough about Dawn to be so supportive about our trip.

Dawn went to school every day the rest of 1979. As she gained strength, I gained confidence that she had no cancer and put that fear in the back of my mind.

As Christmas came and the year drew to a close, I looked forward to the New Year 1980. The new year got off to a good start, for on January 16th Dave and I flew to Hawaii. We were excited when we said good-bye to our children at the airport that morning. Neither of us had flown in a big jet airplane before. The nine-hour ride from Chicago to Honolulu was a very exciting experience.

The first thing I did when we checked in at the hotel at Waikiki was call my pen pal, Patty. I'll never forget how surprised I was when she said her name Patty Patao. I realized that I had been pronouncing her last name wrong for so many years. It was so good to hear her voice after reading her letters for twenty- one years.

Dave and I spent five days on each of the islands of Oahu, Maui, and the big island Hawaii. They were the happiest days of my life.

The five days we spent in Honolulu consisted mostly of time on the beach and tours around the island. We were captivated by the beauty and mood of their culture. After we had been there four days, I said to Dave, "I feel guilty; I haven't thought about the kids at all since we've been here."

"Don't feel guilty. They'll be fine. I'm glad to see you happy and enjoying yourself. I always knew you'd be different if I got you away." When we got to Maui, we headed right for my pen pal's house. We hit it off from the time we met. We talked about our lives and the things we weren't able to relate to each other in our letters. While there, we spent much time together touring the island. It was especially nice to have our personal Hawaiian guide. When we left Maui, we found it very hard to say good-bye, knowing it would probably be many more years before we'd see each other again.The time we spent on the island of Hawaii was quite awesome. The volcanoes and black-sand beaches were unbelievable. On January 29th, we celebrated my birthday. I spent time during the day swimming in the pool. It seemed so strange, being from Michigan, to be swimming in a pool with eighty-degree air temperature. Dave took me out for a romantic dinner that evening at a beachside restaurant. That is one birthday that will always hold special memories. The trip home on January 30th wasn't as exciting as was the one going. All the way home, we talked about the trip and the fun things we did. Now, I was starting to miss the kids but wished I didn't have to come back to all the worries. This trip was like a second honeymoon for Dave and me. We had the chance to be together in a romantic area without the reminders of our problems at home.There is the old saying, "Out of sight, out of mind." That's how I felt about Dawn's illness. While we were in Hawaii, I pretended that she was home as a healthy, happy teenager. When I was with her, I had to face the reality that she had very serious health problems. In my prayers, I thanked God for giving us the chance to go to Hawaii, feeling God cleared my mind of worry so that I could enjoy the pleasure of Dave's company, which I hadn't been able to do for a long time. I decided on the way home to hold those memories in my heart, to recall when things were going poorly.

When we got back from Hawaii, we found Dawn with a rash on her face, and there was concern right away. After a few days of watching it get worse, we decided to take her to Dr. Hayden, our family doctor. He said she had poison ivy.

Her poison ivy cleared up in time, but I worried constantly during that time. I noticed a lot of changes in her as the weeks went by—wetting the bed, wandering around during the night, being really talkative at times, and getting into things like a small child. All these signs could be shunt trouble, but—on the other hand—it might just be part of the damage done by the radiation.

I tried not to worry but with little success. Each morning during devotions, I kept asking God to help me control my fear.

In one especially trying episode, Dawn lit a fire in the fireplace with the damper closed while were all outside. When I came into the house and noticed all the smoke, I panicked. I called out to Dawn. She answered me right away saying, "What?" I went into the living room and noticed paper burning in the fireplace.

I asked her about the fire. She seemed unaware that she had done something very dangerous. Although I tried to tell her about the danger of what she did, it didn't seem to register. I lay awake that night thinking about what was happening to her. She didn't seem to be anywhere near her age level. Sometimes she acted and did things like a four-year-old child instead of being like fifthteen year old she was.

I decided to keep track of Dawn's changing personality by recording all her changes in a little notebook. Some days she would be hyper, some days talkative, some really quiet and distant, and some restless. Sometimes she seemed normal. We never knew what to expect from one day to the next.

In May it was necessary to keep her out of school a week because she was so hyper and erratic. I couldn't get her to be still, even at night. Several nights I was up trying to get her back into bed. She had her bed torn apart and games from the closet out on the floor.

I left Dawn with mom while working because She was always willing to help out. by letting her stay there while I worked.

I suspected that she had pressure from the shunt being plugged up again.

By June 11th, I was worried enough to take her to see Dr. Gracias. He also thought Dawn's shunt could be plugged, so he ordered a CAT scan for June 27th.

When I told Dawn she'd have to have another CAT scan, she started crying, saying, "Ma, please don't take me to the hospital again!"

Dawn's fear of going to the hospital was so bad that I talked to the school psychologist about it. She said Dawn's teachers noticed that she was afraid of something. After discussing her problems at length, the psychologist suggested that I seek counseling for her.

Dave and I talked about Dawn's fear of going to the hospital. We decided to cancel the CAT scan and just keep a close eye on her. Some days she seemed to be very good, and then other days she'd be in one of her personality changes.

We continued to live with the fear of the unknown, trying to deal with it through Scripture. I kept looking for Bible verses that would give me courage to face each day.

Dawn seemed better once we told her that there would be no CAT scan. Things went along pretty well until July 11th when she began sleeping a lot. She'd sleep all night and half the day. I knew that her wanting to sleep so much could also mean shunt trouble.

On July 15th, I awakened to find her wandering around. Her bed was wet, and she seemed very restless. As Dave was laid off from work, I went to work, and he stayed with her.

I was a nervous wreck all day, because it appeared that Dave would be calling about Dawn. The way she was acting that morning was scary.

At 4:15 p.m., I was called to the phone. The voice on the other end was Dave's saying, "Marilyn, I took Dawn to the hospital emergency. You'd better come over here."

When I got to the emergency examination room, where Dave and Dawn were, I found Dawn talking. She said, "Hi, Ma, what am I here for?" She laughed as she talked, like she really didn't understand what was going on. The CAT scanner was a few blocks away from the hospital, so Dave and I drove her over there. We had been there so often that the receptionist recognized Dawn the minute we walked in. She had done well during the scan, but when we walked out, she started vomiting profusely There was little question in my mind now that she had extreme pressure. Soon after we got her back to the hospital, Dr. Gracias came to tell us the results of the scan. I knew by the look on his face that it wasn't good news. With his head down, he said, "The scan shows the ventricles are full, which means the shunt is plugged. We'll have to do surgery tomorrow."

He explained the reason for the decision he was making about doing surgery the next day. He wanted to do the surgery with his own staff, which meant he'd have to wait until morning. He sent her to the adult ICU and said he wanted me to stay with her overnight because I, of course, knew more about her personality than the nurses."If there is any change in her responsiveness, I want you to call me right away."

I felt very important at that moment. It was surprising that he trusted me to notify him of any change.

I didn't sleep much that night, but I was happy Dawn made it until morning without significant change. Dr. Gracias had to delay another patient's surgery so he could get to hers at 8:00 a.m. I held her hand and prayed for strength until they took her off to surgery for the sixth time.

Dave and I found seats in the family waiting room where we had been many times before. As I sat there waiting for word, my mind wandered back to a happier time, about all the fun Dave and I had in Hawaii. The more those happy thoughts crossed my mind, the more upset I became. My mind kept asking questions. *Why does my little girl have to suffer so? Why is it necessary to always be dealing with medical problems?* So many whys went through my mind that I was afraid to admit all my fears to Dave. When the fears and whys built up, I finally broke into tears, saying to Dave, "Why can't we be happy like we were in Hawaii? He took me in his arms, saying, "I wish there was some way I could make the hurt go away."

Wiping my tears, I admitted that I wanted to leave the reality and live in the fantasy world of our Hawaiian trip. I couldn't understand my feelings about not wanting to deal with Dawn's problems anymore, yet wanting to protect her.

Dave and I sat in silence until Dr. Gracias came walking through the door. The first thing I did was try to read his face. Walking toward us, he said, "Dawn came through the surgery okay. She is doing fine. The shunt was plugged down by her stomach."

Dawn was taken back to adult ICU, in which all rooms are private. It was good that she'd be in a room by herself, so she wouldn't hear a lot of noise. I wanted her to have every chance for recovery without depression.

Upon arriving at the hospital the next morning, I found Dawn awake and alert and was happy to see her in such good spirits. Dave was all smiles when he told me how well she had been doing. She was already taking liquids.

On Friday, she was moved out to Pediatrics Main, where she had a roommate and television. The rest of her recovery went well with only minor setbacks. It appeared her recovery this time was her best so far. The only thing that bothered me was that when she talked, she'd sometimes mix past with present. Not understanding why this was happening, I tried to shrug it off.

Her recovery went so well that we had her home on July 23rd, eight days after surgery. Her actions the first night home were very confusing: She talked a lot, but most of it was not true and didn't make much sense. She was restless and didn't want to go to bed until 11:00 p.m. that night. Even after she did go to bed, she was restless and I was up with her most of the night. When morning finally came, I helped her get dressed and took her to my mom's. As I drove to work, I stared out of the window, not really watching the road. I was very bewildered thinking about Dawn's future. As I thought about how she had been the past year, it was clear that her growth and maturity were at a standstill. So many questions kept going through my mind, and I wondered who I could turn for some answers. I wished I knew one of her doctors well enough to tell him about my fears. Anytime I'm around them, there is the feeling they're in a hurry and too busy to listen.

By the time I reached work, I was so engrossed in thought that I wondered how I got there. My head was aching when I punched the time clock, thinking I'd have to be there for eight hours. *Lord,* I thought, *please help me make it through the day. Please help me take my mind off her problems. I can't solve them today.*

In the days following, Dawn seemed more confused and at times disoriented. Many nights I'd wake up to find her wandering around or tearing her wet bed apart. We had many conversations, but much of the time she talked about things in the past. Some days she'd get depressed and very angry. She was having a hard time understanding what was happening to her.

The last week in July, she went with us on our annual campout at Gun Lake. Even though we've been there every year for the past eight years, she got turned around every time she left the campsite.

One day, she took off on her bike and didn't come back for a long time. I got worried, so everyone started looking for her. Dave and I had circled the park a couple times when we saw a man carrying her to our campsite. Panic set in as I raced toward them.

We learned that she had fallen off her bike and hit her head on the pavement. She was full of anger because of the fall and the fact that she couldn't find her way back. The man found her crying and tried to ask her which campsite she was from. She tried to tell him, but was too confused to do so. He assumed she was confused because of the fall on her head.

We ended up taking her to the nearest hospital emergency for stitches on her forehead above the eye. As she lay there on the table, I held her hand and watched her eye movement. She didn't say much, but her eyes told me how depressed she was. She cried and jerked when the doctor used a long needle to freeze the area, preparing it for stitches. She had seen so many needles that one couldn't help feeling empathy with her.

The ride back to camp was a quick one. I knew by the way Dawn was acting that she was mad about the whole ordeal. She has been around doctors and hospitals so much that even getting stitches was a big deal for her.

In August, she went to camp twice. First she went to our United Methodist camp for "special people." She had a good time, and from what she said, she got along fine. Her second trip to camp was the cancer Special Days over by Jackson, Michigan.

She really enjoyed going to camp. Even though I worried about her, it appeared best to let her go. This camp was also for a week and ended just before Labor Day.

The day I picked her up after camp was a big disappointment. Rosemary, a friend from our cancer group who goes to camp as a counselor, gave me an earful when I picked Dawn up at Rosemary's house. She spoke with a sympathetic voice but was concerned because of the extra work that was caused.

She told me Dawn was disoriented but very talkative. She didn't sleep much at night and every morning her bed and clothing were soaking wet. The statements were surprising, even though they should not have been so much so. I wanted so badly to believe everything went okay.

Dawn greeted me with a big hug and acted very hyper, so I knew something was wrong.

On the way home, Dawn was very talkative about camp. She even sang their camp song for me. Bitterness started to creep into my thoughts again. *Since Dawn has such a beautiful personality, why does it have to be destroyed by brain damage?* There was also a good possibility that the shunt was plugging up again. The pressure could be causing her to act like that.

That night after Dawn was in bed, I was lying on the couch watching a movie. They showed some scenes of the Pacific Ocean. It reminded me so much of Hawaii that I started to cry. Dave noticed and asked what was wrong. I said, "We had so much fun in Hawaii that I didn't worry about Dawn at all. If only it could be that way here!"

He put his arms around me and gently said, "But, honey, that was a fantasy world we were in while we were there."

"I know," I said, "but it was so nice to be there and think that all was well with Dawn back home."

After a good cry, I went to bed and thanked God again for the memories and the fact that Dawn was still alive. It was necessary for me to remind myself now and then that many parents have lost their children to cancer. Many parents in our cancer group had already gone through the painful ordeal of death. After every visit with those parents at the funeral home, the thought would come: *Will I have to go through this painful process?*

Hope for the Future

When the kids went back to school in September, things had changed a little at our house. Sherry, a friend of Lori, came to live with us. She had come to me and told about the problems she had at home. We talked many times for hours. She had graduated from high school in June, just before her eighteenth birthday, so she was old enough to make her own decisions. She wanted to live with us, and after hearing the story of her life at home, Dave and I decided to let her.

At first, everything went all right; however, after Sherry had been with us a while, she started demanding a lot of my time. I tried to talk with her as much as I could, but she really got out of hand. After we'd go to bed at night, she would get up and wander around, making noise until I'd hear her. This went on for quite some time before I caught on to the fact that she was jealous of the attention I had to give Dawn. Sherry felt she had to find ways to get my attention, too.

The problems with Dawn weren't getting any better, and now Sherry's psychological problems—stemming from her past—had to be dealt with also. I didn't realize when we agreed to let Sherry live with us that she had so many problems. By the time I did, there was a feeling of commitment to help her. She needed a lot of love, and I wanted to share with her the love our family had available to give.

Sherry got along fine with all three of our kids—to a point. Lori started dating Mark at the end of September, and after that I noticed Sherry didn't want to do much with Lori. At times they even got into arguments like sisters. Sherry needed so much of my attention that for a while I was able to think of something besides Dawn's illness.

Sherry was very good about taking Dawn places and doing things with her. I felt extremely good about that. Most of her friends didn't have anything to do with her anymore because of her immature mental level.

———————•———————

When Dawn went to see Dr. Gracias in September for her checkup, he said the valve on her shunt wasn't pumping very well. In that case, fluid builds up and causes pressure. It appeared that was why Dawn got *so* restless and talkative.

The doctors had been talking for some time about putting Dawn on hormone pills. They said she needed thyroid medication, so they started her on that. They also suggested she be given a female hormone pill to help her develop and go into puberty. I wasn't in favor of that too much because I didn't think her mind was mature enough to handle menstruation. I was also afraid of it because of having heard so much about female hormones causing cancer. Dr. Gracias said there was time to think about it awhile.

———————•———————

After Dawn had been on thyroid medication a while, she seemed to perk up and be more alert. Just about the time she seemed to be doing better, she started slipping backward again. She began coming home from school wanting to sleep all evening and not wanting to get up in the morning. She wouldn't eat supper, saying that her stomach hurt. At times she would get hyper and not want to sleep at all. Several times I found her bed wet and each time wanted to cry out of frustration.

I finally decided to go to school and talk to the teacher about her staying out of school one day a week. They told me they had a lot of trouble keeping her attention so they went along with the idea.

By the time I was ready to leave school, it was time for it to let out. I decided to have Dawn ride home with me instead of on the bus. When she opened the locker to get her jacket, I was surprised at the number of old lunch bags there. I looked into them and found dried up sandwiches and untouched fruit.

"Dawn, why are all these lunch bags in here with food in them?"

"I wasn't hungry," was her simple reply.

"But, Dawn, no wonder you don't feel good half the time. You don't eat at home, and now I'm finding out you don't eat at school either. You're never going to build up any strength this way."

"But I'm not hungry, and nothing tastes good."

I threw my hands up in the air and said, "Please help me, Lord. What am I going to do?" As I cleaned out the locker, I found unfinished math papers and notes that were never brought home. After looking through the papers, I wondered what was happening to Dawn's memory.

I walked back and talked to one of her teachers. The teacher said she felt school was getting increasingly difficult for Dawn and wasn't sure what new things to try with her. I felt very discouraged when we finished our conversation.

In the weeks to come, Dawn's personality was on a constantly changing scale. She became very critical of Lori and D. J. This was unlike her. She usually got along with them well. One of the reasons she argued with D. J. so much was because she noticed he was getting as big as she was. She kept reminding him that she was older.

It was hard for Dave and me to see her as a fourteen-year-old girl, because she acted like a small child part of the time. D. J. was eleven so, when I had to leave the house, I told him to keep an eye on her. I had to make sure she didn't hear me, though. One time she did hear me and said, "Ma, I'm older. D. J. isn't going to boss me around." I knew, after that, I had to make sure that I did my best to help her feel her age even though she wasn't able to act it.

Sherry continued to show an interest in Dawn, taking her to visit her friends and relatives and even to a movie now and then. I could see Dawn turning away from Lori and wanting to spend more time with either Sherry or me. I believed one of the reasons was we were a little more patient with her drastic personality switches.

Besides the personality conflicts, Dawn continued to complain off and on about headaches and stomachaches. She cried a lot over the least little thing. I was becoming increasingly concerned about why all this was going on. I felt there had to be a reason.

The day I really got scared was when Dawn got up from the couch with wet slacks after watching TV. I said to her, "Did you wet your clothes?"

She quickly snapped, "No." I felt her clothes and the couch and found they both were very wet. I was angry inside, but my heart told me she didn't know what she was doing.

I called the nurse at school the next day, only to be tormented by what she had to tell me. She said, "Oh, Mrs. Smith, I'm glad you called. Dawn has been disoriented lately. She can't seem to find her way to her classes. She cried yesterday, calling out for you." These things she had to tell me were a surprise— to a degree.

After hanging up the phone, I sat and cried, trying to release my frustrations.

Dave and I talked that night about calling the doctor. It appeared she was having problems because of pressure from the shunt's failure again.

The next day, December 5th, I took Dawn to see Dr. Taylor. After checking her shunt and hearing about her recent situation, he said, "I want you to take her right to the hospital. I want to run several tests, so we can check some things out."

When we told Dawn we were taking her to the hospital, she stayed very quiet. Her only remark was, "My stomach hurts."

When we arrived there, we had to go through the routine process of going over Dawn's medical history with the interns and nurses. I wised up and each time Dawn went to the hospital after that, I had her medical history right before me in a notebook. It's hard to keep going over the same information every time. It was upsetting to go back each time, recalling her entire history.

A CAT scan was done in the afternoon. When Dr. Gracias stopped by that evening, he had already seen the results. Dawn had been quiet all day, but when Dr. Gracias got there, she switched to being hyper. He couldn't get over how talkative and restless she seemed.

"Dawn, how do you feel?"

"I feel all right," she responded with a slight laugh.

I told him how she had been quiet all day and that she had just changed moods but I wasn't able to make him understand what I was talking about. It was very hard to understand Dawn's moods unless you were with her every day and could see how quickly she could change from one mood to another.

Dr. Gracias told us the scan was good, so there was no problem with the shunt. He said they would do blood tests and skull and chest X-rays. He went on to say, "We'll check every possible problem, but I must admit, right now we are all puzzled about her condition. I really don't know what to check after that." I did not want to believe Dawn had a recurrence of cancer but wanted more tests thinking it had to be something else.

Dawn was in the hospital until December 9th, when they decided to let her go home. Dr. Taylor talked to me about the results of all the tests they did. He said they couldn't find anything wrong with Dawn other than the fact that she was so hyper the whole time she was there. The doctors and nurses were not used to seeing her that way. They usually saw her quiet and depressed. Dr. Taylor said, "We decided to increase her Dilantin from 150 mg. to 200 mg. a day. Maybe that will calm her down some." I was disappointed that he didn't have any solutions but was glad to be taking her home.

On Dawn's first night at home, we were awakened by Lori and Dawn coming into our room. Dawn was crying. Lori said, "Mom, Dawn wants you. She is scared." Lori was annoyed that Dawn had woke her up. She left wanting me to take care of Dawn's crying.

Dave and I both tried to give her the comfort she needed while we tried to find out what was wrong. She said, "I'm afraid of getting cancer again." I was surprised by her fear and tried to hide my own, telling her she was going to be all right. I felt bad for her and did not want to increase her fear by being negative.

The next night while watching TV, she burst into tears. She wouldn't talk to me, so we went to her room where we would be alone. After many tears and lots of talking, she finally told me what was wrong. She said, "Mom, I'm afraid I am going to die. Is my shunt working?" I reassured her it was and that she wasn't going to die. She then surprised me by saying, "I know if I die, I'll go to live with Jesus, but I don't want to die right now." I put my arms around her, trying to assure her that there was nothing wrong with not wanting to go live with Jesus yet.

So many times she was childlike, but her understanding of life and death was mature. After talking and praying with her for some time, she finally went to sleep. My heart was heavy. I didn't want her worrying about death.

The next few weeks, Dawn's fear of pain and death increased. An aide from school called me, saying, "Mrs. Smith, Dawn seems to be terribly upset about dying." I thought she only became scared at night. After talking to the aide for some time, it appeared best to have Dawn talk to Joel, a counselor from the Advisory Center for Teens, which counsels families that have a child with a terminal illness. Joel lost a teenage son to cancer, so she could well relate to the fears a family goes through.

I wanted Dawn, as much as possible, to be like other kids—just going to school and having a good time—not worrying about death.

Dawn saw Joel a couple of times, which seemed to help. I also shared with Joel my feelings, including the desire to take Dawn to another hospital for a second opinion on her condition. Joel agreed that, if I had any doubts, I should get another opinion.

With the holidays approaching, I expected Dawn to perk up and get excited about Christmas like the other kids. Instead she continued to lie around in a real sluggish condition. Her appetite was so poor that she continued to lose weight and was slowly slipping away.

Dave and I sat down after the holidays and talked about taking Dawn to another hospital. He didn't really like the idea but said I could go ahead. He let me know, though, that he thought I was going to be disappointed.

I talked to Dr. Taylor about our decision to seek another opinion. He was supportive and said he'd contact a doctor at University Hospital in Ann Arbor.

A few days later, he called to tell me that Dawn had an appointment to see a neurosurgeon on February 27th. I needed someone else to tell us whether or not Dawn would be this way the rest of her life.

By February 27th, Dawn's weight was down to sixty-four pounds, and she wanted to lie around and sleep most of the time. She had missed too much school to keep up. She'd often ask if her shunt was working, indicating that she worried about it a lot.

The two-and-a-half-hour trip to Ann Arbor was a quiet one. Dawn slept most of the way, and Dave and I were each deep in thought. I prayed that God would guide the doctors and enable them to give us the answers we needed.

We felt lost in that large hospital. It was difficult to find our way around.

We went first to the office of a pediatrician. A resident doctor took Dawn's history. I showed him a typewritten report that I had prepared.

After he read the report, the doctor asked a few questions and then called in the doctor in charge. He examined Dawn and ordered some blood tests and a CAT scan.

After the CAT scan, the neurosurgeon examined her. He pushed on her shunt and said it wasn't pumping very well. He said, "You folks go have some lunch, and then this afternoon we'll talk about the results of the tests we did today."

It seemed like hours before we got to talk to the doctors. When we finally did, I watched their facial expressions which showed frowns of concern as they talked. They said they found the Dilantin level in Dawn's blood to be high. They said they wanted to cut her Dilantin down for a week and then have her come back for a week of tests. The CAT scan showed the shunt to be working and that no surgery was indicated. That was a relief, even though they said the shunt was sluggish.

They suspected Dawn's pituitary gland wasn't working, explaining that the pituitary gland is the master gland that controls hormone function and that it could be damaged.

They also said that Dawn had to go back and spend a week going through tests. The look on her face indicated that such news didn't go over with her very well.

Dawn didn't want to go back, but after I explained how important it was to her future, she helped me pack her clothes and favorite stuffed animals.

On Monday, March 9th, we went back to Ann Arbor to spend a week. Dawn was admitted to Mott Children's Hospital at 9:30 a.m. in the morning. At 11:30 a.m., we were still waiting for a room.

Once we got settled in Dawn's room, we found the nursing staff to be very friendly and helpful. They showed us around the floor, which housed all teenage patients. I was impressed with all the patient activities available. They even had a classroom for those who wanted help in keeping up with school work.

It didn't take long to get settled in and get acquainted with the mother of Dawn's roommate. They were from Jackson, Michigan. She, too, was staying there with her daughter.

The nurses helped make up a bed with chairs by Dawn's bed so I could stay by her. I got food from the cafeteria for myself so I could eat with her. I was allowed to eat her food and buy her something from the cafeteria if she didn't like the food on her tray.

The first couple days, the routine tests were done. On Wednesday, tests were done by a psychologist and a specialist from the endocrinology department.

After the tests the endocrinologist, Dr. Cline, explained some of his findings and ideas about her problems.

Dr. Cline said Dawn had radiation damage to the hypothalamus. The appetite, behavior, and emotions are controlled by that part of the brain. He also said she needed more thyroid and hormone replacement.

After discussing the matter at some length, I understood a little better why Dawn acted the way she did. He said he'd have to do quite a few tests to prove his theory and decide if they could do something to help her. Dawn questioned me about what the doctor said. I tried to explain the tests without worrying her too much. I could see that just hearing the word *test* meant bad news to her. The look on her face was always the same when hearing the word tests. She would have a angry look and the not make eye contact and always turn away from me.

On Thursday, Dawn went through more psychological tests and had a spinal tap. After the spinal tap, she had a backache and just wanted to lie in bed. I tried to keep her mind off it, but she looked at me with resentment in her eyes. That look was her blaming me for letting the doctors order tests that caused her pain. I finally gave up and went for a walk around the halls.

Glancing in some of the rooms, I could see some pretty serious problems. Two kids with broken necks. There was children from around the state going through tests. At Butterworth, everyone who I had met while Dawn was in knew why his or her child was there. Spending time in a hospital is hard, but it makes you realize that you are not the only one going through turmoil because of medical problems.

When I returned to Dawn's room, a psychologist asked to talk with me. Again I went to the conference room to listen. She showed me a lot of test results that indicated Dawn was working only at a sixth-grade level at school. She said she also discovered, through tests, that Dawn's maturity was also on a child's level. After discussing all the test results with me, she asked, "Are you prepared to take care of Dawn the rest of her life?"

"Why, yes. Why do you ask?"

"Because Dawn will never be independent enough to leave home."

I explained to her that even though I didn't like hearing it, I had come to the conclusion myself that she'd never gain independence. She did not have normal development over the last five years so I knew in my heart that it was the radiation damage but hoping it would't be as bad as it is.

After talking with me, the psychologist commented on my dedication to taking care of Dawn, something I took for granted. She said she sees a lot of kids from broken homes with parents who aren't willing to assume responsibility for taking care of a problem child.

I was shocked by all the things she told me. She said, "You're a special mother. Dawn is lucky." I feel God gave me Dawn and my other two children with no guarantees that raising them would be easy. I let her know that Dawn would be my responsibility for life, if that's what she needed.

That night when I tried to sleep, the events and conversations of the day kept going through my mind. I was more concerned about how Dawn would accept her disabilities. She so often talked about how she wanted to grow up and become a nurse. How would she ever accept the fact that she would never be a nurse? I morned the fact that Dawn had been such a smart, active and caring person already at nine years old. Now having to except that she could never be the nurse or anything else she may have wanted to do.

On our last day at the hospital, Friday, the doctor wanted to do a test in which an IV entry would have to be used. Blood had to be taken from her vein every half hour for four hours. She was taken to a treatment room so a resident doctor could start the tests. I explained to the doctor that Dawn's veins were hard to find, making IVs difficult to start. He said that starting IVs was no problem for him.

I was supposed to wait in Dawn's room while the doctor got the IV ready, but a short time later the doctor came and got me. He said he was having trouble getting a good vein, and there wasn't a nurse available to help him. I wanted to say"I told you so," but I kept quiet. I was thankful he decided to let me be there to help.

The process of starting an IV ended up taking an hour and a half, with all three of us becoming very frustrated. The doctor tried every vein in Dawn's arms, legs, and feet. Dawn was very good, though, during the whole process. I could see the pain in her eyes. Every time I saw the needle go in and not work, I cried inside for her.

When the doctor finally did get a vein to work, which was in her foot, he said, "Dawn, don't move your leg even a bit because the needle might pull out."

She spoke right up for the first time, saying, "Do you think I want to go through this again?" The doctor and I looked at each other and smiled, knowing she had a right to be upset.

She never moved a bit for the four hours they took blood from her. When the test was over, she eagerly got ready to go home. The doctors released her at 8:00 p.m. She was tired but ready to go home instead of staying another night.

I felt so good about all I had learned during the week that telling Dave about everything was easy. Both of us rejoiced over the fact the doctors felt that Dawn could have a future free of cancer. They felt that because she had gone six years without a recurrence, she may never have one again. Our biggest concern now was how to cope with the damage from the radiation given to her in 1975.

In the next few weeks after the tests in Ann Arbor, we could slowly see some improvement in Dawn. The doctors had increased her thyroid medication and taken away her Dilantin. This seemed to perk her up enough that she was more able to handle schoolwork.

Dave and I were so happy with Dawn's improvement that we decided to go ahead with plans we had made earlier to take the kids to Disney World in Florida. We made plans and preparations using our pickup camper to make it a family affair. Sherry got permission to be off work so she could go with us.

The trip down was long, because we had so many problems with the truck— first a flat tire and then an overheated-radiator problem. By the time we arrived at a KOA campground in northern Florida, the kids were fighting because of being in the pickup camper so long. We discovered that Dawn had wet several times, her clothes and the bunk where the kids had been sleeping. I had a lot of laundry to do when we arrived but tried not to make Dawn feel any worse by saying alot. Lori and Sherry had already said quite enough.

Dawn felt embarrassed and kept saying, "I can't help it." Not understanding why she had those spells, I wasn't sure how to help her overcome them, When going to Disney World got a wheelchair for Dawn so she wouldn't get tired walking. She cried in embarasement riding around in it so often tried to get out. She didn't talk to us; only make sounds. That got very frustrating for all of us.

At the end of the day Dawn was withdrawn and uncooperative. Being at Disney World was supposed to be a lot of fun for her, but it didn't turn out that way. We were glad to get her back to the camper.

The rest of the week got even worse. We stayed in Tampa with our friends Ken and Judy for four days. Three of those days Dawn wouldn't talk or eat. We couldn't even get her to take liquids. Every time I tried to put food or liquids to her mouth, she clamped her teeth together. I worried about her wetting on Judy's furniture, so every few hours I walked with her into the bathroom. She would stiffen out and cry like I was hurting her. She also didn't seem to be sleeping much at night, for every time I looked at her she'd be staring into space. The look in her eyes was frightening. Everyone tried talking to her, but there was no response.

Finally on the third day, I couldn't take any more. We were all supposed to go to Busch Gardens, but I decided to stay behind and take Dawn to a doctor.

Judy made an appointment for Dawn to see their family doctor. After he checked her all over, he tried asking her questions that she could give yes or no answers to. He said her body was dehydrating because of not eating and drinking enough fluids. He gave me some pills to relax her stomach saying she was tensed up. It was hard to give the doctor much of her history in such a short time, He did explain, in some detail her personality switches which helped me to understand her better.

The doctor reassured me that Dawn should be okay and that the trip home shouldn't be a problem. I was relieved to hear that. Dawn also seemed more relaxed when the doctor finished explaining many things to us.

Judy and I took her to McDonald's and got her favorite meal. Happily, she finally started to eat and drink a little. The next few hours after we ate, we spent time talking a lot to her and finally got out of her that she was mad. I discovered that she didn't get along very well with the other kids in the camper on the way down. She was also angry about not being strong enough to walk around Disney World.

That evening and the next few days Dawn completely changed. She talked, ate, and took part in things we did on the way home. Naturally, we were all happy about the change but couldn't help but wonder what caused it and why she finally came out of it. Was it the doctor's talk, the pills, or did she decide to quit being mad? The answer to these questions will never be known.

We had a blowout on the truck on the way home and couldn't find a store open to buy a new tire. We had to travel the last 200 miles with two bum tires and no spare. As a result, we did a lot of praying that we'd arrive home safely, which we did.

We had to take Dawn to Ann Arbor several times in the spring for more tests as an outpatient. When they finished with all the tests, the doctors sat down and explained to me all their findings. Even though I didn't understand a lot of the medical terminology they used, the pieces of the puzzle of Dawn's problems seemed to be fitting into place.

Dr. Cline said that Dawn would need to see an endocrinologist every three months to check the hormones and thyroid level. I didn't want to keep returning to Ann Arbor, so they made arrangements for her to see a Dr. Pool in Grand Rapids.

Dr. Cline said that if Dawn's hormone deficiency problems were corrected, a lot of her problems would disappear.

As a result of the tests done, Dawn was off Dilantin completely but began taking a new kind of thyroid medication, a female hormone pill called Estinyl and cortisol. He said these pills were necessary because the tests proved the pituitary gland, which usually distributes hormones, was nonfunctioning.

I understood the function of the thyroid medication and Estinyl, but the purpose of the cortisol was new to me. He explained that Dawn's adrenal gland, which regulates the stress hormone, was nonfunctioning and that the cortisol would take its place. He stressed the fact that once she started taking this drug she could never miss. This drug was supposed to help her body cope with stress.

Before I left that day, I had to learn how to give Dawn a shot. Dr. Cline said that if Dawn should refuse to take her pills—which she had done sometimes— I'd have to give her a shot of cortisol. It was important that she not miss any dosage. The idea of trying to give her a shot when she was in one of her uncooperative states was very frightening.

A month after Dawn had been on her new hormone schedule, I took her to Dr. Pool for a checkup and was very pleased with the way he talked to her.

He told us there was a lot of research going on in the field of personality change and that it was likely great strides would be made within the next ten years.

I was on a high after we left his office and gave Dawn a big hug and said, "Dawn, you're going to be all right. The doctors are going to find a way to help you." She smiled at me and gave me a big hug back and then said, "I love you, Mom." We were both very happy. I knew she understood a lot of what Dr. Pool had said.

In the following weeks, the hormone therapy seemed to be helping. Dawn started gaining weight, because the cortisol gave her an appetite. It got to the point where I had to watch how much she ate. I hadn't done that in years.

The next time Dawn went to see Dr. Pool, I found out that one of the side effects of cortisol is a buildup of body fluid. He weighed her and discovered that she had gained sixteen pounds in a month's time. He suggested I watch her intake, trying to keep her on a high-protein diet.

Watching Dawn's diet was easy at first. When she went into her hyper, snippy personality, it was harder to control. She would go to the cookie jar, and if I tried to stop her, she'd say, "I'm hungry. I haven't eaten lately." When I tried to explain that she had eaten just before that, she'd get angry and say, "No, I didn't." I found it very hard to convince her that I was keeping her out of the cookies for her own good.

Even with all the problems, it appeared very good that she was on hormone therapy. I was also encouraged every time Dr. Pool saw her. It appeared that finally we had found someone to make her future better.

Dr. Pool gave me hope that in ten years or so the help Dawn needed to live a better life would be available.

I was prepared to take care of her for as long as she needed help. She wanted to be a nurse and help handicapped kids, often talking to me about it. I had to believe that someday her plans could come true. She had been through very much but still had much love to give. *Please be with us, Lord Jesus, and we'll make it.*

Taste of Defeat

In the weeks to come, Dawn's personality changes worsened. She continued to show signs of several different ones. I couldn't leave her at home alone, even though she was now sixteen years old.

The bedwetting and the wandering around at night also became more frequent. One night when I was putting her to bed, she kept screaming at me, "I'm in the wrong room! This is D. J.'s room! This is not my bed, either!" I was surprised that she was that confused. It took me a long time to settle her down and convince her that she was in the right bed.

Soon after Dawn was in her hyper personality, she went into her quiet, withdrawn one. It was always difficult to get her to eat and take her pills when she was this way. The one and only time I gave her cortisol as a shot was a terrible scene. First, I tried my best to get the pill down her. When that failed, Lori had to help me hold her down to give the shot. If anyone had walked in, it would have appeared that Lori and I were about to commit murder. Lori held Dawn's arm down while I held her legs down and poked the needle in the upper part of her leg. She screamed and tried to kick the whole time.

I felt so bad when it was all over that I said I'd never give her a shot again. I felt there had to be another way. Later on, when Dawn was like that, I happened to be around my friend Barb. She suggested I put the pill on a spoon with some water and hold Dawn's head back and force it down that way. That scene wasn't very nice either. Dawn screamed and cried, leaving me with a fear of her choking.

Another problem was she refused to eat or drink when she was like this. One time she got so dehydrated that when Dr. Pool saw her he said, "She's like a dried-up prune." I wanted so badly for him to give me some miracle advice, but he didn't have any. He said for me to force fluids down her and not worry about the rest.

Her school called, telling me about their problems with her. She sat in school and stared a lot. When she was in her hyper personality, she'd be all over the school. One time, they had to go out of her unit to find her.

Many times her talk was very confused when she was hyper. She would go on about things that were either from the past or didn't make sense at all.

These personality problems caused her to miss a lot of school, because it wasn't practicable to send her to school when she was so uncooperative.

I kept praying, "Please, dear Lord, help me to handle these problems. Heal her so she can be normal like her friends."

In May, Lori went to the prom with her boyfriend, Mark. She looked beautiful all dressed up. I tried to visualize what Dawn would look like if she'd been able to grow like Lori. I also compared Dawn to kids her age, wondering if she would have been as pretty and happy as some of them.

In June, when Lori graduated from high school, I found myself all caught up in the happiness of that day. We had a big open house for her. Dawn was in her restless, talkative personality that day. She kept wandering around eating and talking to people. It was hard for some of our friends, who we didn't see very often, to believe me when I told them how Dawn's personality changed. I guess it would be hard for me to believe, too, if I didn't live with it all the time.

A week after Lori's graduation, we received an unexpected call from Butterworth Hospital Emergency. Lori and I had gone to a graduation open house. While we were gone, Dave went for a ride on his motorcycle. The call came soon after Lori and I arrived home. The phone rang and Lori answered it. I heard her say, "Yeah, that's my dad. Do you want to talk to my mom?" When she yelled that it was Butterworth Hospital on the phone, I went running.

The nurse on the line told me Dave had hurt his leg and that I should come down to the hospital. Both Lori and Sherry wanted to go with me. I didn't want Sherry to feel bad by my choosing Lori over her, so both of them stayed home with Dawn and D. J. while I went alone.

I was upset all the way to the hospital and kept praying that he wasn't badly hurt. My nerves couldn't take many more problems. Dealing with Dawn's and Sherry's emotional problems was about the limit.

When I arrived at the hospital and found Dave, he told me his bike had fallen on his leg when he turned the corner on the expressway ramp. The doctor taking care of him said that Dave's leg was badly broken and required surgery.

The next day, I found myself sitting in the family waiting room, waiting for another operation. Memories of Dawn's operations kept racing through my mind. I tried to keep those thoughts out, but the effort was unsuccessful.

Dave came through the surgery well, despite the fact that it took nine pins and a plate to hold the leg together. The doctor made it very clear that he had no use for motorcycles.

Later in the day, my mom and dad brought Dawn up to see Dave. When I left her that morning, she was talking and in a normal personality. Now she seemed to be very withdrawn. When she was in the room to see her father, she stared at him and muttered in a scary way.

Dave was very sleepy from the surgery and was lying in bed with his leg up in a sling. I guess, to Dawn, it did look pretty awful. I couldn't do anything with her while she was there.

Dave was in the hospital for seventeen days. During that time we celebrated our nineteenth wedding anniversary. I went to the hospital after work that day. I was upset because of an incident at work, so when I arrived at Dave's room I was crying. I continued crying while I told him about what had happened. Some anniversary day it was—he was lying in a hospital bed, and I was crying.

Our kids walked in with my mom and dad. They had their hands full. Lori and Sherry were carrying presents while Mom carried a cake. Dave and I were quite surprised and happy. I soon cheered up and forgot about my day at work.

Dawn was still in a withdrawn state, but she seemed to know what was going on. The nurses let us cut the cake and enjoy it there with Dave. Even though the hospital isn't a fun place to celebrate an anniversary, our kids surely helped us make the best of it.

Dawn continued her withdrawn state for eleven days. During that time, I took the kids camping with our church group, without really wanting to go—with Dawn acting the way she was. It turned out well, because I got so much encouragement from many church members.

The camping trip turned out to be a lot of work for me and a real eye-opener for my church family. Most of the members did not realize Dawn's personality was changing so, much less seeing her so withdrawn.

She couldn't be left alone, so my friend Barb helped me. The hardest part was at mealtime. Dawn would not eat anything. Begging and pleading were tried without results. She just stared and shook her head. When everything I tried failed, it resulted in a helpless feeling. It was embarrassing to have to force her pills down. She made a big fuss, so people naturally wanted to know what was going on.

After the pill-taking session, Dawn looked at me with much hurt and confusion in her eyes. I looked into her eyes, saying, "Oh, Dawn, I wish I knew what's going on. I'd give anything to be able to understand you and help you." I took her in my arms, holding her close, crying inside. I loved her so much and wanted so badly to help her.

By the time Dave came home from the hospital, Dawn was back to her normal personality. He couldn't get around very well, so I saw an opportunity to keep Dawn busy getting things for him. It also helped me keep track of her without her realizing it.

In August she went to the cancer camp. When I picked Dawn up, Joel, who had been a counselor there, said Dawn had been very hyper and talkative while at camp. She said Dawn didn't sleep well at night, and her bed was always wet in the morning. The most surprising thing she told me was one night Dawn got up to go to the bathroom and never came back. Joel got worried and went looking for her. When she couldn't find any sign of her, she got more worried, thinking perhaps she had walked into the lake.

After a thorough search of the cabins the second time, she was found. Joel was very surprised to find her sleeping in a bunk with a boy.

The story was that the boy tried to tell his counselor that there was a girl in his bed, but because the boy was noted to be a comic, what he said was shrugged off as an attention-getter. Because Dawn's memory was not good, she had returned to the wrong cabin and, therefore, to the wrong bed. She thought someone was in her bed, so she just climbed in.

Joel told me the whole camp had a few laughs the next day, but they had all been worried before she was found.

I laughed at what Joel had told me but hid my real feelings. As Dawn's mother, it was hard to hear she acted like a small child when she was sixteen years old.

I kept praying to God for guidance in handling all the ups and downs in my life. Some days it appeared things were going pretty well. Other days I felt like giving up. Still, I had the assurance that God loved me and understood me. I've been thankful that, through these past few years, I have found a personal relationship with Him. When reading His Word and praying in the morning, I could feel His presence.

Dawn went into what should have been the eleventh grade at school in September. Her personality changes, bedwetting, and medical problems seemed to get harder to handle. She missed quite a bit of school before Christmas because of them.

Dave and I were disappointed that he was still home on medical leave, but if it had to happen, at least one good thing came out of it; He was able to be home with Dawn. Some days I came home from work and found him upset because she had been so hard to keep track of. He was always able to sleep at night when Dawn was up wandering around. I was the light sleeper who heard her every time she got up.

Sherry and Lori always heard her, too, because they slept in the same room. Some nights I'd wake up to hear Sherry yelling, "Dawn, will you get back in bed? I have to get some sleep."

Then Dawn would sass back, "I don't have to!" By that time I'd be up. I had to get after her in order to get her back in bed.

Her being up at night got so bad that I resorted to giving her some sleeping pills. The pills seemed to slow her down but didn't keep her sleeping all night as I had hoped.

The teachers at school had just as much trouble with her as we did at home. When she was in her hyper personality, she'd be sassy. Then when she'd change to her withdrawn one, she'd sit and stare all day without any communication. Of course, while in the personality I like to call *normal,* she acted more like a girl her age. She'd be so sweet and loving during that time that it was hard to believe she could act like any of the other personalities she showed.

When she went into what I called her talkative personality, she would talk nonstop. She would mention a lot of things that happened in her past, frequently not remembering recent things. The family enjoyed being around her when she was like that, because most of the time she was a comic, too.

Christmas that year turned out to be the best time we'd had in months. Dawn was in her normal personality for most of the holiday season. She was very happy on Christmas Day, and so was I, realizing that there was much to be thankful for, even though things could turn bad again soon. At least our Christmas came and went unspoiled.

I said to him, "I really don't think this family should continue supporting Butterworth Hospital."

He smiled, saying, "Well, let's not."

I hugged him and said, "If only it could be that simple."

The new year got off to a good start with Dawn going to the winter cancer camp. She was in her normal personality when she left and was still the same when she came back. When I picked her up, counselor Rosemary told me about what a great time Dawn had. It was pleasing to hear Rosemary talk about all the things Dawn had participated in.

After hearing Rosemary's report and seeing the happiness on Dawn's face, I was glad she had gone.

There were so few things that she had been able to take part in, I was happy and thankful that this camping trip turned out so well. All the way home she sang her camp songs and told me about the things she had done.

When she was like this, I fantasized her being a healthy, happy teenager with years of happiness ahead of her.

The good days came to an end, with the bad ones coming back, as in the past. In February, she had a couple of bad weeks where she was totally out of control. I received a call from school that crushed me. The voice on the other end said, "Mrs. Smith, Dawn is completely uncontrollable here at school. We'd like you to keep her home until she's better."

I told the lady on the phone that we'd keep Dawn home but what wasn't said was not how I felt. What I really wanted to say was, "Don't you understand that Dawn can't help it when she's like this?" But, why should I have expected the school to understand

Dawn and be attentive to her needs when it was difficult, even for me, to continually remember that she was not a normal girl and had little hope of ever becoming such. I guess I expected the school to know how to handle her when she got this way. I hated to keep her out of school every time her personality changed.

During the time she was home, she did things that you'd expect a two-year-old to do.

I came home one night and found her room a mess from games she had gotten out, and some were even destroyed. Trying to talk and reason with her about what she was doing brought no results. She got really sassy and said, "They are my games. If I want to wreck them, I can." I cleaned up the mess and, while picking up the pieces of her games, cried out, "Lord, this isn't Dawn doing this. It's someone else in her body. The Dawn I know is the one who showers me with kisses and hugs."

After Dave had been with Dawn for several days, I was glad to be home the following day. She was awake most of the night, talking and wandering around, so I didn't get much sleep.

Like Dave, I found myself keeping busy just following her around. I had to get her out of Lori's makeup, the papers in the desk, and again from things in her room, but this time it was stuff that belonged to Lori and Sherry.

Reverend Barker came out to talk to Dave and me about the problems we were experiencing with Sherry. While he was talking to us, I noticed Dawn under the card table in the family room. She had lots of papers and was just throwing them around. Reverend Barker and Dave were doing most of the talking, so they didn't notice my attention was on her and not on the conversation.

I continued to observe her and noticed at times she'd cry. She seemed to be in another world.

I asked Dawn what she was doing under the table, but all I got was a whiny, "I don't know."

I knew there was no sense in trying to figure out why she was acting like this, so I said, "Come here, Dawn." I took her in my arms and held her close. She was still the size of ten year old, cuddling me like a two year old but reality was she was sixteen. Holding me tight she continued to cry. When I asked what was wrong, she shook her head and said, "I don't know."

I then said, "Do you miss school?"

She said, "Yes."

It was clear that she could not understand why she did the things she did. She didn't seem to remember the different changes, so I didn't see how she could understand them. I kept thinking about all the things that were happening to her for which there were no answers. One of the teachers at school told me that Dawn acted normal and that she was a good student, especially in reading. Then another day I'm told how bad she was and how they couldn't get her to do anything. Her papers would be handed in all scribbled up.

By the end of March, the problems with Dawn, Sherry and Dave not working got to be so much that tension built up between Dave and I. There was also the stress from him not working. His leg was healed, but he had a bad limp. Dave could not go back to work because he found out people were laid off. He was unsure if he wanted to look for another factory job. After much discussion, we decided to go to Florida and look into being campground managers. Having a job working together would make it easier to take care of Dawn. The way things had been going, she was going to need a lot of care. Lori and Sherry took charge of the house and DJ while we were gone. I was concerned about problems they might have with Dawn but Dave said, "Don't worry, they'll be all right." I was thankful that my parents lived next door so they could oversee everything. Dave and I really needed a chance to get away by ourselves, so we looked forward to the trip. We returned from our trip feeling rested but disappointed because the campground job we looked into didn't turn out to be what we wanted. Lori and Sherry told us dealing with Dawn while we were gone was difficult. Sherry said that at first Dawn was good, so she could take her various places. A few days after we left Dawn started acting up. She wouldn't eat, talk, or take her pills. They both tried giving her the pills, but she kicked and screamed. They felt she was upset because we had left her. I tried talking to Dawn about her feelings but she just stared. While holding her I said, Dawn please be OK, you need to eat and take your pills." Trying to see if I could get her to tell me how she felt, was unsuccessful. She would not respond to me either; she just stared. I took her in my arms and said, "Dawn, please be okay. You've got to eat and take your pills." I couldn't get her to eat, but I fought with her until I got her to take her pills.

The next few weeks were a nightmare. Dawn continued to have all kinds of problems. She complained of stomachaches, headaches, double vision, and loss of bladder and bowel control. We finally had to buy some adult diapers and protective panties, because she wet so often during the day. She was angry and embarrassed, crying when I'd put them on her. I tried to explain why I was having her wear them, but that made no difference. I felt bad for her, because I knew she couldn't help it. However, I couldn't keep cleaning the furniture and floor and washing a lot of clothes and bedding. It was just too much to keep up with. I felt like everything was caving in on me. Sherry came back to see us after she left. I knew she wanted our attention and love, but she couldn't handle sharing us with Dawn's problems. Both girls needed lots of attention for different reasons.

At the end of April, Dave was scheduled for a minor surgical procedure. The night before he went in, Dawn was awake most of the time. Every time I touched her, she screamed as if she were in terrible pain. I tried asking her if she was in pain, but she wouldn't say anything.

I had planned to leave Dawn with my parents while I went to the hospital to be with Dave. When I tried to get her up and dressed, she kicked and screamed, "No, no!"

I said, "Dawn, do you hurt anywhere?"

Still screaming, she said, "Yes."

My mom was standing there, feeling helpless. I turned to her and said, "I'm taking her to the hospital and having her checked. I can't take any more of this."

She continued to scream while I tried to dress her and get her to the car. I didn't know what to think, having never seen her act this badly. Dr. Gracias told me he'd meet me at the hospital.

Instead of going up to Dave's room to see him before surgery, I found myself sitting down in the emergency room with Dawn where I had been so many times before.

The emergency attendants were surprised with Dawn's actions. She screamed and kicked through their examination of her. When Dr. Gracias got there, he ordered a CAT scan.

By the time I got up to see Dave, he was already in surgery. I went to the family waiting room to wait for the doctor. I wasn't there long before he came and told me Dave was fine and would be in recovery for a while.

I went downstairs to see Dawn, who was still acting very hyper and uncooperative.

Dr. Gracias came back a short time later and said the scan was okay. Even though I was relieved, he couldn't tell me what was causing her to act as she did.

Dr. Gracias left right after our talk. The emergency doctor came and said that Dawn would be admitted for tests.

When I inquired about the tests that were going to be done, no one knew anything. I knew, with Dawn's being admitted on Friday, there wasn't a lot they'd do soon, because it was a weekend. Naturally, I was frustrated because of the day's events and Dawn's actions. I didn't want to keep her at the hospital, if nothing could be done at that time.

I called Dr. Taylor, her pediatrician. He said he had no plans to run tests and that she was admitted because of what the emergency doctor said had happened there. I couldn't see Dawn staying at the hospital, so when Dr. Taylor said I could take her home I decided to do so the following day.

I went between Dave's and Dawn's rooms the rest of the day. When I told Dave what had happened with Dawn, he was surprised and felt bad he was not with me. I reassured him that was okay, knowing that he and Dawn would both be coming home the next day.

I had struggled with Dawn to get her to the hospital, and the next day I struggled with her to get her out. She screamed, kicked, and held on to the bed when I tried to get her up. I was surprised because she was usually happy to leave the hospital. With the help of a nurse, I got her dressed and out to the car. She screamed all the way. People going by us didn't know what to think. I felt embarrassed, because I was afraid they might think I was hurting her.

From the time I brought her home on May 1st until May 6th, she continued with her uncooperative state of not eating or talking. She also continued to wet the bed and lie around during the day.

Then on May 6th, she suddenly changed to a restless and talkative mood. The one surprising thing about the change this time was that when she walked, she dragged her right foot. This was strange, because it seemed to happen overnight. I asked her often if she had hurt her leg, but she kept saying no. When I left for work that morning, I was upset and drove with my mind in a daze. I came up too closely behind a car that was going to turn. I put my foot on the brake and turned to the right, barely missing a ditch. When turning back onto the road and just missing a car head-on, I ended up with the back end of my car hitting a post. I was so scared that I just sat there and shook awhile. The lady in the other car stopped to see if I was all right. She said, "I can't believe you didn't hit me." I told her I was surprised, too. I went on to work, thanking God all the way that I was more or less okay.

I tried to take my mind off Dawn, but I kept seeing more changes in her. She wouldn't use her right hand to eat, and she would sit around more instead of trying to walk.

On Sunday, May 9th, Dawn was outside walking on the porch when I heard a thud and then crying. By the time I got out there Dave had picked her up off the ground.

Dave checked her over and said he thought she was okay. She had scratches on her face, but other than being scared, she seemed to be all right.

When I arrived home from work Monday night, I found Dawn on the couch, lying on her back with her feet on the floor. I asked her why she didn't sit up straight. "I can't," was her reply. She was talkative and later she left the couch, dragging her leg even more Because of the fall, her leg, and the fact she was still wetting her clothes, I told Dave I would call Dr. Taylor. I felt there had to be something wrong that she didn't want to walk.

As it turned out, Dr. Taylor called me Tuesday morning to see how Dawn had been doing since she left the hospital. After I told him what had been happening, he wanted me to bring her right in.

After his examination, he was so concerned about her condition that he made arrangements for me to take her to Dr. VanDyke, a neurologist, that same day. Dr. VanDyke said he wanted to study her old CAT scans. I was very impressed with his concern and examination. He said Dawn could have had a slight stroke, and there was a possibility that she might even have a tumor.

The idea of her having another tumor was scary and difficult to believe. I went home and told Dave what the doctor had said and how worried I was. Dave wouldn't say much. But I could tell by the blank look on his face that he was a little worried now too.

On Friday, Dr. VanDyke called and said he wanted Dawn admitted to the hospital on Monday so she could have an angiogram on Tuesday. Fear came over me, because I knew Dawn would be upset when I told her she was going to the hospital.

I put off telling her until Sunday night. She had changed from her talkative, restless state to her quiet one. When I tucked her into bed, I talked to her about her problems. I then said, "Dawn, you've got to go back to the hospital tomorrow, so the doctors can do a test." As soon as I said the word *test*, she started crying.

Holding her in my arms, I tried to give her the comfort she needed. I felt so sick inside about having to upset her like this. She cried out, "Mom, please don't make me go back there." Her words made me cry. Only God knows this hurt me as much as it upset her.

Through the night I thought about what was to come, wishing it were possible to run away with Dawn and save her from all the pain she had to go through. I wanted to run off and live in a fantasy world and be able to spare her the misery that goes with her condition.

After these thoughts of doing something irrational, I prayed that God would put those dumb thoughts out of my mind and give me the strength to show Dawn a strong, supportive mother.

On Monday, May 17th, Dawn was again admitted to Butterworth Hospital for tests. For the first time, I wasn't the one taking her. I had to work, so I used that as an excuse not to be the one putting her in.

Dave and Lori took her that day, and I went over there after work. Dave had already left by the time I arrived, but Lori told me what a rough day it had been. Dawn wouldn't eat, get up, or walk. I tried to talk to her, but she wanted to be left alone.

On Tuesday morning, my devotions really spoke to me. They were about a lady who had lost her best friend through death. Even though she was saddened—because of the death of her friend— she decided it was better to have known her for a short time than not to have known her at all. I wondered if God was preparing me for the results of Dawn's tests. I had lived with the knowledge that we could lose her. But this devotion helped me to see how lucky we had been to have had her longer than the doctors first expected back in 1975. My spiritual life had become much stronger because of the problems I'd had to endure.

An angiogram was done on Dawn in the morning, and that evening Dr. VanDyke came and told me the results. I had mixed feelings when he said, "She has a mass on the left side of the brain in the area of the shunt." I was relieved that he thought the mass was a cyst and not a tumor but scared because even a cyst is very serious.

Dr. VanDyke said the next step would be to have a CAT scan done. I wondered right away why the mass didn't show up on the scan that was done a couple of weeks ago and how I would explain to Dawn why another scan was going to be done so soon.

On Wednesday, Dawn was sleepy most of the day. When she wasn't sleeping, she was whining, and my telling her about the scan didn't help. I couldn't get her to walk other than to the bathroom. She kept complaining that her arm and leg hurt. The nurse also discovered that she was running a fever of 101 degrees. I really worried about what was going on. I'd seen her get so depressed in the past that it kept her from getting well, so I wondered if this was happening again.

Dawn was so upset on Thursday morning when she went for her scan that she was first given a sedative.

I went to work after the scan, and Dave stayed with Dawn. Later that night when I came back, Dave had gone home. When one of the nurses saw me, I heard her say to the head nurse, "Here comes Dawn's mother." The head nurse told me that Dr. Gracias was waiting in the hospital to see me. I panicked. I didn't know he had been consulted, so I figured surgery might be what this was all about.

It wasn't long until Dr. Gracias and Meridell, his nursing consultant, appeared on the pediatrics floor. I tried to read their faces as they approached me. He confirmed my fears by saying he wanted to operate on Dawn the following morning. He said he thought Dawn had a cyst that should be removed right away. I was very much frightened and upset by his news, but told him how confident I was in his decision. My biggest concern was telling Dawn and seeing her reaction. After I related those feelings to Dr. Gracias, he and Meridell agreed to go with me, so he could tell her about the surgery.

Dr. Gracias was very gentle when he told Dawn. She didn't show any signs of being afraid. After he left, Dawn said to me, "Mom, I know Dr. Gracias will make me better." With that, I started crying as I held her close. She had so much confidence in Dr. Gracias, because he had always been there when she needed him. My tears were fear of another surgery and wishing I knew what Dawn was thinking. She seemed so strong but was she? With her mind I wondered if she understood was was going to happen.

When Dave and I arrived at Dawn's bedside in the morning, we found her awake and alert. She didn't show any signs of fear until the nurse came with the sedative to put her to sleep. Then the reality of what was coming starkly hit her. She started crying. She sobed and took my had with a strong grip. While holding her in my arms, I talked again about the surgery, hoping to give her the assurance she needed. Reverend Barker came to be with us and had an opportunity to lead us in prayer when we needed it most.

After Dawn was taken to surgery, we quietly walked to the family waiting room where we had been so many times before. I thought, as we walked through the door, *How many times do we have to go through this?*

Reverend Barker brought along some devotional material, but I couldn't keep my mind on it, thinking mostly about what Dr. Gracias had said the night before. One of the complications that he talked about was the possibility of the cyst's bursting during surgery and the consequent possibility of losing Dawn during the process. The thought of that happening was too much.

We spent most of the two hours it took for the surgery talking about Dawn and telling Reverend Barker what a delightful little girl she had been before all her problems. It was enjoyable to tell him about all the fun times we remembered having with her. We talked about how Dawn always wanted to be a leader and help other kids at school. Even when she went to special education she wanted to help by pushing the wheelchair of a boy she called her friend. I laughed at the time she got mixed up at Cancer camp and was found in the wrong bed with a boy. She insisted that he was in the wrong bed and not her.

While we talked, I had one eye on the door, so I could get a look at Dr. Gracias' face when he came walking through. My prayer was that he would come walking through with a smile on his face, saying, "Everything went well. Dawn is fine."

The Valley of Death

Even though the surgery took only two hours, it seemed much more time had passed before Dr. Gracias came through the door. I jumped up when I saw him, trying to read his face as he walked toward us. He asked us to join him in the conference room, just off the waiting room. As Reverend Barker, Dave, and I followed him in there, I thought, *Oh no, it must be bad.* He had a frown on his face and he did not make eye contact when waking into the room.

Dr. Gracias struggled with his emotions as he said, "Dawn came through the surgery fine, but what I thought was a cyst was a tumor. I removed only part of the tumor because it was in her speech area. I didn't want to destroy that."

I cried out, "No, not another tumor. I can't go through that again." I was standing turning away with my hands on my face. I cried with a scream then paced the floor in a small circle.

Dave grabbed me to give me support as Dr. Gracias told us all the grim details. I fought back the tears when he said, "The most merciful thing we can do for Dawn now is to do nothing." He explained that she couldn't have any more radiation and chemotherapy would do little to slow down the tumor.

I felt as though I had been asked to go back in time and relive the horror of that first tumor. Only this time we would not have the hope of treatment. I was stunned by everything that was being said. When Dave and Dr. Gracias finished talking, Reverend Barker led us in prayer. When Reverend Barker had finished, I could tell by the expression so sad with his head down on Dr. Gracias' face that he was hurting as badly as we were. I thought how hard it must be for him, after all these years of being able to help Dawn, to tell us now that he couldn't do anything more.

Some of our family had stopped by while Dawn was in surgery to see how things were going. When Dr. Gracias left, we still had to face them. I was crying so hard I didn't know how I could get the news out.

Dave continued to hold me up as we walked out to give our family the news. They took it as hard as I had. We talked and cried for some time. All the while I was trying to convince myself it was all a bad dream. I couldn't believe God would let this happen after all Dawn had been through. Even with all the faith I had gained the last few years, at this time I was angry and asked, "Why, God? Dawn doesn't deserve this."

When Dawn was brought to the pediatric intensive care unit, we dried our eyes so we could see her. The nurses were very good about letting my family go in to see her, even though it was supposed to be restricted to parents and grandparents.

Dave and I went in to see her first. I took one look at the bandage on her head then turned to Dave and cried. She looked like my sleeping beauty. She lay there in such a peaceful sleep with no look of pain. *She can't have cancer again.* I left the room crying hysterically.

Dave and I sat quietly by Dawn's bed all evening. She woke up a few times, looking to see if we were there. Each time she woke up, I kissed her, telling her how well she was doing. I knew she was doing well when she asked for a chocolate shake. It was too soon after surgery for her to have one, but just the fact that she asked was encouraging. So many times in the past she was too depressed after surgery to want anything.

At 12:30 a.m., Dawn was doing so well that the nurses talked Dave and me into going home. I felt very drained, so the idea of sleeping in my bed sounded good. The nurse assigned to Dawn promised to let us know if there was any change during the night.

Even though I went home to sleep, I was awake most of the night. I couldn't stop thinking about the news Dr. Gracias had given us. I wanted so badly to believe it was all a bad dream. I kept asking why. It just didn't make sense for this to be happening again.

The next morning, I arrived at the hospital before Dawn awoke. I bent over to kiss her just as she woke up. She smiled and said, "Hi, Mom." I responded to her cheerful voice with a hug, kiss, and my best smile, even though I was hurting badly inside.

Many doctors came by to check on her, including Dr. Gracias. By the time he came, Dawn was sitting up in a chair while the nurse changed the bed. She gave him a big smile, saying, "Hi, Dr. Gracias." He was surprised to see her so alert. He smiled back, saying, "Dawn, it's nice to see you sitting up already."

She was really doing well. Usually after surgery she'd be depressed and wanted to be left alone. I felt the extra cortisol she was given before surgery helped her body cope with the stress. In the past, when she had had surgery, we didn't know that her body wasn't producing the adrenalin it needed to help her stand the strain.

After Dr. Gracias examined Dawn, we went out into the hall to talk. She hadn't been moving her arm and leg on the right side, which had me quite concerned. When I questioned him about it, he confirmed what I already suspected. He said her right side was paralyzed because of the tumor. He went on, saying, "Mrs. Smith, when you take Dawn home, help her to enjoy the time she has left in her life. Don't hold back from doing things you think she'd enjoy." While we talked, I tried to stay calm, but inside I hated him for what he was advising. I wasn't ready to think about her *dying*. I felt hate that he was telling me Dawn was going to die. There seemed no sadnes in his voice, just wanting me to face reality.

Earlier in the morning, Dr. VanDyke had been by to see Dawn. He said Dave and I should talk to a doctor who specializes in oncology about giving her chemotherapy. When I told Dr. Gracias this, he said, "You can talk to a doctor about it, but it may do her more harm than good." Even though I wanted to believe that chemotherapy could cure her, I knew he was right about the dangers.

Dawn was in good spirits all day. It was so nice to see her like this, and then all of a sudden her mood changed. She fussed when the nurse tried to give her liquids, and when it was time for her to get back into the chair, she became angry. I thought, *Oh no, here we go again with another personality switch.*

Sunday morning, I woke up with a headache. Upon arriving at the hospital and finding Dawn staring, it got worse. Dr. Gracias came by and was surprised to see the change in Dawn from yesterday. He—like me—didn't want to see her go through a depression. He said she was doing well enough that she could move out of ICU into a room where she could have television. That helped to perk her up a little, but most of the time she spent in silence and appeared to be thinking a lot. I felt I should talk to her about the cancer, but I just couldn't bring myself to do it. I wanted her to think about getting well so she could go home. I was afraid that if I talked to her about cancer and the possibility of chemotherapy she might go into a deep depression.

I was not able to spend as much time as I wanted with Dawn, because I had to go back to work. While at work, I thought about her and would wonder how she was doing. It was hard to concentrate or appear to be cheerful. I was thankful that my coworkers and steady customers were very understanding. Each day after work, I would go to the hospital with a headache. There was a lot to do in preparation for her coming home.

Even though Dawn was making a good recovery from her surgery, it was obvious that the new tumor had done more damage. She could no longer get around by herself. She didn't ask to use the bathroom. And now she seemed even more confused about past and present events.

On Friday night, May 28th, one week after surgery, Dave and I met with Dr. Dykstra, an oncologist. I was hoping that he could give us some encouraging advice. He talked to us for some time, going over Dawn's history and what the outcome might be if he tried treating her with chemotherapy. Perhaps one of the most important things he told us was that if she had chemo she would be prone to infection. Because she had a shunt and a history of becoming infected, it could easily happen again while on chemo. Another problem was her history of poor eating habits, and then there was the difficulty of personality changes. He said it was very important for a patient on chemo to eat a good, balanced diet; this was something we couldn't control with her. When she was in her withdrawn state, we could barely get her to take her pills and liquids, much less a balanced meal.

Even if Dawn didn't have all these problems, he said there was still the reality that the chemo might only slow the tumor down for a short time. The hard fact was that the best treatment for a brain tumor is radiation, and she had already had all her body could tolerate.

After weighing all the pros and cons of chemo, Dave and I realized that the doctor was really trying to tell us to do nothing. I could tell by the sadness in his voice and the frown on his face that he had the same feeling as Dr. Gracias. We had put her through so much already, there was little point in adding to her misery.

Seeing our disappointment, Dr. Dykstra said, "If Dawn does real well for the next few weeks after she goes home, bring her back to see me, and I'll reevaluate her case." Fighting back tears of defeat, Dave and I thanked him for the time he spent arriving at his decision. We said we'd let him know if things changed. But I knew it would take a miracle from God to free Dawn of all her problems.

When we returned to her room, I was still fighting back tears and emotion. It was now harder to face her, knowing what we did. Dave and I were in agreement about not telling her anything. A whole week had gone by since surgery, and she hadn't asked us why she could no longer walk and use her right hand. She had apparently just accepted it.

While talking with Dawn that night, we found her to be mixed up about events of the past again. Dawn spent most of the evening talking about things that didn't jibe with what was now going on. When Dave and I tried to correct her about some events, she became angry at our disbelief. Listening to her talk helped me to realize why she hadn't asked us more about her condition. She had been here so much that she was confusing one hospital stay with another.

On the way home, Dave and I discussed our decision not to tell Dawn about the tumor. After seeing her confusion that night, we felt better about keeping it from her. She was adjusting to her new disabilities and seemed to be content most of the time. If we were to tell her about the tumor today, the chances were she'd forget about it tomorrow. We were dealing with the mind of a small child, not one of a seventeen-year-old girl.

Memorial Day weekend was a very difficult one to get through. With Dawn in the hospital, we didn't plan anything special. I packed a picnic lunch to take to the hospital. My mom and dad met Dave, Lori, D.J., and me there. We got special permission to take Dawn outside, in her wheelchair, to the park across the street. We didn't want to celebrate the holiday sitting inside the hospital.

The weather was warm, sunny, and a little breezy. When we told Dawn we were taking her outside to the park, she became very excited. We all enjoyed our picnic with her so much that we hated to take her back inside. As I sat on the grass, I kept looking at the blue sky and thinking, *Are we going to lose Dawn to our God in heaven above? Will we have to remember her next year on Memorial Day as many families are remembering their departed members today?*

That night when I went to bed, I lay awake thinking about Dawn and the meaning of Memorial Day. All my life, this day had been just another holiday. This year it was different; now I was thinking about all the parents who have lost a child through untimely death. I didn't want to give my child up. The thought of it was just too much to endure. I talked to God about my feelings until I fell asleep. Each time I woke up, I started again. There was a burning desire inside that wanted to make sure God was listening.

During the next five days, there was much to do, and time went by very fast. Between working and being at the hospital, I saw Lori and D.J. only the one time they visited Dawn and a few minutes at night before they went to bed.

Dawn's moods changed to a great degree. I was never sure what to expect each day when I got there to see her. One evening I spent talking to her about her fight for life. She had the "I want to give up" look in her eyes. I told her how important it was that she kept that strong will to live, like she'd shown in the past. With the old problems combined with the new ones, especially the paralysis, it was particularly important that she have a strong desire to get well. All the time I talked, she kept those blue piercing eyes of hers staring right at me without saying a word. Finally, when I finished, she said, "I want to live, Mom." I put my arms around her and gave her a big hug and kiss. I then held her hands in mine and prayed that God would heal her and give us both the strength to endure whatever occurred in her life.

When I left the hospital, I was sure that she understood more about her condition than I was ready to admit. Even though I wanted to protect her from worry, she knew things weren't the same. She especially didn't like having to wear the adult diaper called depends. Even though I had explained to her several times why it had to be used, it was degrading to her. I had a terrible headache by the time I arrived home just thinking about all the changes. We had taken Dawn to the hospital with walking ability we brought her home confined to a wheelchair. It was bound to take a lot of adjusting for all of us.

Connie, one of the hospital's social workers, visited with Dawn and me several times so as to prepare me for Dawn's homecoming.

She helped a lot by taking time to answer my many questions. In the past, when Dawn had been in the hospital, she had improved, and then the day came when she walked out on her own. This time it was going to be very different.

Dave and I were thankful the day Connie told us she had made arrangements with Dave's health insurance company to pay for all of Dawn's homecare needs. We were overjoyed to learn his insurance policy included homecare coverage.

Connie said our coverage was so good it would pay 100 percent of all costs, which included a nurse eight hours a day, a hospital bed, a wheelchair, depends diapers, and a home physical therapist. I was so thankful to hear this news that I felt God had lifted one of the big burdens off our shoulders. I took a minute right then to say, "Thank you, Lord, for watching over us."

The big day finally came on Friday, June 4th. Dawn came home. The nursing staff all stopped in her room before we left to say goodbye and wish her continued progress. I felt mixed emotions when Dave and I walked out the hospital doors with Dawn in a wheelchair—happy to be taking her home but with fear that we'd be bringing her back. Since part of the tumor was still lurking in her brain, recovery as in the past appeared quite tenuous.

Several members of my family were at our house, waiting to greet Dawn as soon as we arrived. She had been quiet all the way home, being a bit depressed and tired but as soon as we got her in the house, she opened up with a smile, saying, "It's good to be home."

The hospital bed, wheelchair, and everything else we needed were there waiting. Dawn was tired, so she wanted to get right into bed. She was happy when Dave showed her the controls so she could position the bed where she wanted it. We put the bed in the family room, right by our kitchen, and put a television where she could see it from the bed. I wanted her to feel comfortable and be where I'd be spending most of my time when I was home.

I had to leave for work soon after Dawn was settled in. The evening at work seemed to drag, because my mind kept wandering back home. When I got home from work at 10:30 p.m., Dawn was still awake and alert. She seemed as happy to see me as I was her. Dave said the evening went well and the nurses that would be taking care of Dawn had come out to meet her. I felt a little resentful that I wouldn't be taking care of her. Also wondering how they would cope with her personality changes, and her not wanting to take her pills. The nursing director from the homecare nursing service had said the gals they were sending over would be experienced with problem patients. A few days after Dawn came home, Dave and I went to Nashville, Tennessee. We had plans with friends, made hotel reservations and bought tickets for a country awards show in advance. My family was all for Dave's and my getting away, so offered to take care of Dawn. The trip turned out to be a fun and relaxing time. Our friends, Linda and Dave, were good company and helped to take my mind off my problems. It was a welcome change from the pressures of the last few months. Being many miles away from Dawn made it easy to fantasize her being well and happy. Dave was happy to see me relaxed enough to be laughing.

The first two weeks that Dawn was home went very well. One of the nurses, Kim, really took to Dawn. She went out of her way to make Dawn comfortable and keep her entertained. She was very willing to take Dawn outside for fresh-air rides in her wheelchair. This so reassured me that I felt able to go to work. Knowing that someone would be with Dawn and ready to give her good care made a great difference. My time at home was always filled caring for her. There was a lot to do in taking care of her, but God was supplying sufficient energy. I wanted my time with her to be special without overly protecting her.

One of the things I enjoyed doing most for Dawn was helping her to the bathroom. It was too much effort to put her in the wheelchair each time she had to go. When I picked her up off the bed, she would put her arms around my neck, holding me tight. Sometimes she even played with my hair. I felt such closeness to her during these times. Dave worried about me hurting my back. I reassured him that I was picking her up in a way that would protect it. I said to him, "Please, Dave, don't deny me the joy and warmth I feel when Dawn puts her arms around me." It didn't take him long to see the increasing bond between Dawn and me, so he gave up trying to stop me from carrying her.

Nancy, the physical therapist who came twice a week, taught me a lot of techniques for getting Dawn in and out of both the bed and wheelchair. At first Dawn was very cooperative with Nancy. The therapy seemed to be helping. With Nancy's assistance she started walking. I got so excited that I worked a lot with Dawn in the evening and switched from carrying her to the bathroom to walking her. The more I praised Dawn about walking, the more response I got from her. We were both very happy.

On June 21st, she switched personalities. When I arrived home from work, I found a note from Sue, one of the nurses. She wrote that Dawn seemed upset all day and gave her a hard time while getting her dressed for the day, which had to be done by force. Sue also wrote that Dawn wouldn't eat or take her pills. I was angry by the time I finished reading the note. I thought Sue was trained to handle these problems. I got the pills myself and, by force, got Dawn to take them.

After reading a note from Nancy, I was even more frustrated. She said she was unable to do any physical therapy with Dawn, because she kicked and cried with every movement. I felt so discouraged, because this showed how hard it was for even trained people to handle Dawn when she was uncooperative.

The rest of the week didn't go much better. The two days Nurse Kim was here, she somehow got Dawn to eat and take her pills. On the days Nurse Sue was there, she did nothing. She just left me a note telling me how bad Dawn was. I found out from my mother that on Wednesday morning Sue was late. Mom happened to stop by, finding Dawn all by herself. When Mom walked in, she found her crying. Mom checked her, and found Dawn and the bed to be sopping wet. Mom called the nursing service. They said Kim was sick, and Sue was supposed to hurry out. Evidently she did not do so.

I was very upset by the end of the week and asked the nursing service to take Sue off Dawn's case. They agreed this would be for the best.

Many of our church members were going camping for the weekend. We looked forward to going on our annual camping trip with other church members. this trip each year. Even though Dawn was giving all of us a hard time, we decided to take her and go anyway. That turned out to be a lot of work. She wouldn't cooperate with anything I tried getting her to do and never uttered a word while we were gone. knowing the cancer was in the speech area of the brain I collapsed from being tired and worried apone arriving home. As I looked at Dawn asleep in bed, my mind went wild with thoughts of the cancer being active again.

Shortly after that, Dawn stopped speaking and wouldn't talk no matter what we did to encourage her. My dreams were mostly nightmares of her dying while I stood by helplessly. On Monday morning, I was awakened from one of those dreams by Dawn's low-sounding cry. As I came rushing downstairs, I found her paralyzed arm and leg hanging outside the bed railing. She was so badly wedged in that I screamed for Dave to come and help. This was upsetting to me, and I said to Dave, "She's getting worse. She's losing control of her limbs, and she's not talking."

He tried to calm me down by saying, "You've got to accept what's going to happen."

Dave and I deal with our feelings so differently that it was hard to talk to each other about them. He accepts things more graciously than I do. I just couldn't believe Dawn was going to die, even though I could clearly see her slow deterioration.

When I returned from work that night, my niece Tammy, who is a year younger than Dawn, was over to see her. I talked to Tammy about what had happened in the morning and my fears that Dawn wasn't talking because of the cancer. When Tammy and I finished talking, she walked over to Dawn and kidded with her until she started laughing. I was surprised and happy to see Dawn having a moment of joy.

Just before Dawn's appointment with Dr. Pool for her hormone level checkup, she switched personalities to a very withdrawn state. By the time we arrived at Dr. Pool's office, it had been several days since she had eaten. All I could do for her was to get the pills down her throat by force. Dr. Pool was shocked by her condition and ordered an increase in her cortisol dosage. Because Dawn had to go through her regular blood tests, I took her downstairs in a wheelchair. I had a hard time moving her around, because of lack of experience in pushing a wheelchair. It surely made me stop and think about all the people who have dealt with wheelchairs for years.

Dave and I talked about Dr. Pool's suggestion of calling Dr. Gracias. We agreed that if we did he'd probably put her in the hospital. Neither one of us wanted that yet. We wanted her home as long as possible.

During the next five days, her condition continued to worry me. She wanted to sleep a lot and, in order to get her to eat, I had to feed her. At times the food seemed to collect in the side of her mouth, even choking her. After all I went through getting her to eat, several times she couldn't keep it down. The nurses didn't want to take a chance of her choking, so I fed her when I was home.

On Friday night, July 23rd, I put Dawn in the wheelchair and took her over to my folks' house. Some of my other family was there for a birthday party. When Mom got the ice cream out, I decided to give Dawn some, thinking it would be easy for her to swallow. When she finished it, her face turned red, and she started choking. I picked her up and patted her on the back, trying to stop it. I screamed for Dave, and he and everyone else came running. Dave stopped her choking, but her face was still bright red. I touched her arms and chest to discover that she was burning up. Quickly taking her temperature, I discovered she had a fever of 103° and was having spasms.

I called Dr. VanDyke to see what we should do. He said we should take her right to emergency so they could examine her. Willie decided to go with Dawn and me to the hospital. I guess she sensed my insecurity. I sat in the backseat beside Dawn and kept her sponged down with a cold cloth. She lay there with her eyes staring at me, as if asking me what was going on. In between my tears, I explained what was going to happen. My heart felt very heavy. Because she hadn't been able to talk the past few weeks, I also thought about the last time I heard her say "Mom." I'd give anything to be able to hear that again.

Approaching the hospital emergency entrance, I thought, *Here we are again.* Dawn was wheeled right into an examining room. I informed the doctors of her medical history, hoping they wouldn't put her through a lot of routine blood tests.

The doctor wanted to start an IV right away, but after several attempts at trying to find a good vein, he gave it up. He had two other people try, but neither of them had any success.

All the time this was going on, Dawn had tears running from her eyes but couldn't make any sounds. This really bothered me, because I knew the needle pricking hurt her. I hadn't realized until now that she could no longer make sounds. She kept looking at us with eyes that seemed so full of fear. I kept talking in hope of helping her understand what was going on.

By the time we got Dawn to her room and settled in bed, it was after 12:30 a.m. I wanted to stay with her overnight, but because I was wearing shorts and a tank top, I felt cold and out of place. Dave stayed with her, and I took my sister home. It was 3:00 a.m. when I finally got to bed, feeling mentally drained, again asking God why all this was happening there had to be something wrong that she didn't want to walk.

Thinking about Dawn dieing was so unbearable that I tossed and turned most of the night. Even the sleeping pill that my sister Barb gave me didn't help. Many visions of the past danced through my mind, especially the ones that involved happy times. I knew it was not fair for me to want Dawn to live when she could have a home in heaven free of pain. Still, I just couldn't bear the thought of being separated.

On Sunday, a CAT scan was done. The scan proved what we already suspected: The cancer was spreading down the ventricles. Dr. VanDyke said all we could do now was keep her comfortable.

After a couple days of care in ICU, Dawn was moved out into a regular room. Soon after I got to the hospital on Friday, I noticed Dawn's face was bright red. The nurse took her temperature and blood pressure and found them elevated. A while later, the fever and redness of her face went away, and Dawn fell asleep. She looked so relaxed that I decided to go to the coffee shop for lunch.

When I came back to her room forty minutes later, I found the nurse standing over her, checking her blood pressure. Her face was bright red again. I took her hand and asked the nurse what was wrong. She quickly said, "I don't know, but her blood pressure is up again. I'm going to get the resident doctor." Dawn clutched my hand tightly. She started spasming so badly that I became scared. I rang for a nurse, who came rushing. She said Dawn's fever was up extremely high again and started putting wet clothes on Dawn's head.

By the time the resident doctor arrived, I was hysterical. I'd never seen Dawn look so bad. She look so red from the high temp and was lying so still. After he checked her over, he asked me to step into the hallway. He then told me I had to decide if Dawn's heart stopped whether we wanted someone to run in there and start it again. Still crying, I said, "No. Dave and I had agreed we didn't want to keep her alive by machines." He said our decision had to be part of the record in case that should happen.

Dr. Gracias's nurse, Meridell, came by and, seeing how upset I was, said, "Marilyn, go with me for a Coke. You need to get away for a few minutes." I wanted to go back in with Dawn, but I didn't want her to see how upset I was.

Going with Meridell gave me the opportunity to pour out my feelings because I was so uptight inside. She was uncommonly understanding about my fears. By the time we finished talking, I felt like I could go back upstairs and face Dawn and the fearful look in her eyes.

When I went back to Dawn's room, her fever was up to 106°. They put her back in ICU. Kathy one of Dawn's past nurses talked to me, helping me understand what had been happening. I told her it was hard not knowing what Dawn was thinking. Her eyes were the only way she could communicate. Dr. Gracias and Meridell came by and explained that Dawn's fever kept going out of control because the tumor was pressing on the body thermostat. He said, "We'll do everything possible for her pain. That's all we can do." I thanked him for his concern. But inside I cried, because the time had passed for him to be able to help her get well.

When Dave came up, I was under so much stress that I could hardly tell him what had been happening. Kathy stayed beside Dawn while Dave and I stepped out for a few minutes. She sensed my need for a good cry. We went to the parents' waiting room where I felt free to let my tears go. I couldn't hold them in any longer. Dave held me close, saying, "Go ahead, honey, you need to get it all out."

I kept crying out, "But I don't want to give her up."

Stroking my hair, he said, "She's in God's hands. He'll take care of her."

Even though I loved Dave, I resented the fact that he could be so logical about this. I don't think he really understood how watching Dawn deteriorate was tearing me apart. Dave was not the type to discuss his feelings so I was not sure how he felt inside but I am sure it was hard on him too.

Dave and I stayed with Dawn overnight. Dave slept on the cot provided and I slept in the chair by her bed. That's where I wanted to be and knew I wouldn't sleep anyway. So many thoughts kept going through my mind that it was just too busy to sleep. I tried to keep uppermost in my mind that if Dawn died she would be safe in the arms of Jesus. I pictured her, as a whole person, walking along beside Him. I liked to picture her as a beautiful, developed, seventeen-year-old girl with beautiful, long blonde hair. I knew, if she hadn't gotten cancer, that is what she would have been like today. "I love you, Jesus, but please don't take Dawn away from me yet."

In the next few days, Dawn stayed stable enough that she was moved from ICU to a private room. The room was cheerful looking and had a cot I could sleep on. I liked the idea of being able to sleep on a cot right in her room.

While she was in ICU, I spent a lot of time talking to her, even though her only response was her nod and eye contact. So often she looked scared and confused. I kept telling her to put up a fight and she'd get better. I wasn't at all sure that was right, but I couldn't bring myself to do otherwise. Once while I talked, she kept turning the rings on my finger, which seemed to me like a nervous reaction. I said, "Dawn, are you scared?" She nodded yes. Then I said, "Are you afraid you are not going to get well?" She responded quickly with a yes nod again. Not being sure how to answer that, I held her tight, saying, "God will take care of you." I tried to hold back my tears, but the more I thought about her, the more they came. I so wanted to protect her from the pain and fear of the unknown. Our family friend Reverend Doubblestein came by. When I told him about my feelings, he said he'd talk with Dawn. After his visit with her, he reassured me that she understood a lot more than I thought she did. He said he talked about Jesus and her and living with him in heaven, which was something I couldn't do.

Now that Dawn was in a private room with a cot, I wanted to be with Dawn all the time, so make the decision to take a leave from my job. Dr. Taylor saw my need to be with her and agreed it would be better for both Dawn and me if I took a leave.

The people I worked with at D&W Foods were very concerned and offered to help in any way. My manager said I could have a leave for as long as needed.

Relatives and friends responded in the same way. They continued to visit Dawn and me at the hospital, while also offering to help Dave, Lori, and D.J. at home. Mothers from the Living with Cancer group, church family, Pastor and hospital Chaplin Father Bill stopped by at times offering ther suport.

After I stayed at the hospital several nights, Dave convinced me to go home and get some sleep. He agreed to stay right by Dawn and call me if she showed any signs of needing me. I felt tired and depressed and consequently decided maybe a good night's sleep would help.

I thought about Dawn so much during the drive home that my head ached and caused me to feel nauseated. I wanted to talk to someone who could understand my feelings and decided to call our former pastor, Reverend Bud. He knew what I went through in the beginning year of Dawn's illness. Reverend Bud listened to all my fears, but even talking to him did not help, but when I hung up, I had a good cry. Barb walked in about then, giving me the support I needed at that moment. Thinking about Dawn on the way home caused me to feel nauseated.

It was hard to get to sleep after I went to bed. Sometime after I did, I was awakened by the phone at 3:10 a.m. It was Dave telling me to come quickly to the hospital, because Dawn was having a bad time.

I couldn't get there fast enough. I went so far as to get angry with Dave speaking to him very harshly, because he had encouraged me to go home. I was upset all the way there, saying out loud over and over "why did I go." When I walked into Dawn's room, I found him and a nurse sponging Dawn down with a cold cloth. I sat down to hold her hand, while watching her eyes. She again looked scared. Dave and I spent the rest of the night putting cold cloths on her head while rubbing her arms. We kept talking to her so she'd feel our love and not be afraid.

After that night, it was even harder to get me away from her overnight. I felt all I could do for her now was to stay with her. The time I spent with her was precious.

The next couple days, Dawn's condition continued to deteriorate. Every doctor that walked into her room had a different opinion as to how long she could hold out.

On Wednesday night, August 11th, I experienced a very restless night, hearing every move the nurses made in her room. I listened to the beeper on her IV bottle, convinced that the sound would stop if she died. The worst sound of all was hearing a woman crying. I jumped up and ran out into the hall. Just going around the corner was a lady in a wheelchair. My heart pounded fast as fear gripped me.

I was afraid something had happened to the young girl, Shelly, in the room next to Dawn. She was there dying of cancer, too. I checked her room, not hearing anything decided everything must be okay. I went back to Dawn, leaned over the bed kissing her with tears running down my cheeks as I listened to her struggling to breathe. I stooded there crying for some time. The nurse walked in asking if I was all right. With anger inside, I looked up and said "I have to be".

Not knowing quite what to say, she replied, "I know this must be hard for you."

Dawn slept all day on Thursday. I unsuccessfully tried to get her to respond. She was definitely slipping away. The fear of her dying at night haunted me.

Thursday, after spending another restless night listening to Dawn's breathing and not having her respond, I was sure something terrible was happening. By the time Dr. Taylor came around, he confirmed my fears by saying, "I'm sorry, but Dawn is no longer responding." He said she could go on like that for a while. I just couldn't picture myself sitting by her bed, waiting for her to die. I'd always sat waiting for her recovery. Dr. Taylor stayed and talked for quite a while.

After he left, I shut the door to Dawn's room, as if I could shut out the rest of the world. I talked to her in between my tears. I didn't want her to leave me, even though I couldn't do anything to make her life better. The separation was more than I could bear.

I sat staring and thinking for a long time. First, I had to accept Dawn's wheelchair, then her silence. Now I couldn't even look into her eyes. I was feeling hateful. *Why is God letting her die slowly like this? Hasn't she suffered enough?*

It took quite a while before I had enough courage to call home and let Dave know what had happened. Once I called home, word spread rapidly, and the family started coming up to offer support. My dad took the news the hardest. I found myself being the comforter. As he and I cried, he talked about the things he had done with Dawn. Finally I said, "Dad, she's still breathing. That means God could still heal her. We have to hang on to that."

Relatives and friends stopped by during that day and evening. I was mentally and physically exhausted. Everyone did their best to comfort and help me except what was happing while I was thinking they couldn't understand my heartache in losing Dawn this way. To me there was a big, black cloud hanging over my head with no more sunshine.

Even though I now knew Dawn would die, I didn't like the word *death*. It seemed so final. If she had to leave us, I preferred thinking of her death as a transformation from this earthly existence to a life eternal. I could accept her leaving me only by thinking about the fact that I'd be able to join her. I'd talked about my feelings to our new pastor Reverend Peterson and some of my family and friends. The ones that understood best were friends from the cancer group who had already lost children.

I'd thought a lot about how God would answer my prayers. Every day I asked Him for strength to accept whatever outcome He chose for Dawn. "I couldn't believe God was letting her go through this just to put me to the test,"—as one mother put it to me.

I was told by a mother who had a daughter escape injury from an accident, "God knows I'm not strong enough to handle the situation, if anything should happen to my daughter. That's why she's okay." She implied that God must figure I'm a strong person, and that's why I've been chosen to endure all this heartache. I was angry because that lady felt that way. I couldn't believe our loving God chooses certain people to endure such intense pain and heartache.

Accepting God's Call

From that Friday, August 13th, Dawn was in a coma until the following Friday, August 20th, when she passed away. This was the longest, most terrifying week of my life.

The first thing that haunted me was the date—Friday the 13th. There was fear of that date building from the time I realized it was coming up. I had never thought of myself as being superstitious. However, after Dawn slipped into a coma, my mind concluded that there was something sinister about that day.

On Saturday, August 14th, Dave and I hardly said two words to each other. We were upset and didn't want to let on to the other how miserable we really were. I was so afraid of Dawn leaving this world when I wasn't in the room that I wanted to be with her continually.

Dawn's breathing was so poor that each time she took a breath, I was afraid it was her last. The nurses had to clear her mouth often by suction because of the buildup of mucus.

Dave kept after me to take a walk, so that evening I went outside and sat on the grass. Looking into the sky. I asked God to heal Dawn in whichever way was His will. Although not wanting to lose her. It tore me apart as I watched her struggle to take each breath. I cried uncontrollably mixed up about God's will in her life. I wanted someone to explain what part God had in it. Everyone just kept saying, "It's God's will." As the next few days went by, my nerves got worse. Now and then, Dave managed to leave the hospital for a break and be home with the other kids. I'd gotten to the point where I wasn't sure about how much to rely on the views of others.

I found it very hard to sleep in the room, listening to her breathing. On the other hand, the two nights I slept away from her I nearly drove myself crazy wondering what was going on.

A statement from Joel, who had counseled Dawn in the past, helped me most to handle leaving Dawn's room. She said, "Marilyn, Dawn could die while you're in the bathroom. If you're supposed to be with Dawn when she dies, you will be."

On Tuesday, August 17th, a resident doctor came in and checked Dawn, after the nurse was alarmed by a sudden drop in her blood pressure. The doctor said she would be surprised if Dawn made it through the night. Her blood pressure was down, breathing shallow, and body temperature was down to ninety-two degrees. I tried to be brave, but as soon as the doctor left, I put my arms around Dawn and cried out, "Please don't leave me, Dawn. I need you so."

Dave came in, found me crying, and asked what had happened. After I told him, he put his comforting arms around me and said he'd stay with me so I wouldn't be alone.

The night went by slowly. I jumped at every move the nurses made when they came into the room. When Dr. Taylor came by in the morning, Dawn was stable again. He said she could continue like this for some time urging me to leave her room more frequently.

I missed being home with Lori and DJ, but the desire to remain with Dawn in her last few days outweighed the desire to be thirty miles away in Wayland.

Family and friends who lived in Grand Rapids invited me to stay at their place so I did end up staying away a couple of times. Dave stayed with Dawn and promised to call me if there had been any change. I was so tired and apprehensive listening to Dawn's breathing that the short break helped.

On Thursday, August 19th, Dawn had another bad day. Her breathing was very shallow, her body temperature was down to ninety-two degrees, and she had to be suctioned out continuously. My concern about her gave me another terrible headache.

The nurses were very good. They had gotten to know me well enough by now that they could tell by my face whether I was worrying. Dawn's nurses, Wendy and Becky had gotten to know me and were understanding to my feelings. They talked to her like she was listening to them. I realized that they cared about my feelings of wanting to believe Dawn was sleeping and would one day wake up. It was my way of coping.

On that particular day, they made a special effort to warm Dawn up with extra blankets. They also took time talking to me about my sadness of Dawn's body being so cold for I had never felt anyone that cold before.

Dave stayed with me so I wouldn't be alone. I remained with Dawn, and he found some resting place down the hall. During the night I woke up from a dream that Shelly, the little girl in the next room, had died. I saw her mom go screaming down the hall saying, "Shelly is gone." When I woke up, I hurried to Shelly's room to see if she was still there. Finding her there, I went back to check Dawn. I felt terrified. Darkness is very scary. Dawn's shallow breathing didn't help.

On Tuesday, Wednesday, and Thursday, Dawn's condition fluctuated constantly, with changes in her breathing, blood pressure, and temperature.

On Friday, August 20th, I had no idea that this was going to be my last day with Dawn. I sat by her bed all morning trying to read.

At noon, my friend Maryann came to spend the day with me. I told her what had happened and that I wasn't leaving Dawn's room that day. She didn't try to change my mind after listening to Dawn's shallow breathing.

Late in the afternoon as I stood chatting by Dawn's bedside, I noticed her face got very red and that she was struggling for each breath. She acted as if she was in terrible pain. Dr. Bergman, the resident doctor, came right away. They tried very hard to get an IV of manitol started. It took awhile before the drug started working, and Dr. Bergman said that this time it wouldn't help.

After I called Dave and told him what had happened, he raced at eighty miles an hour to get to us. When he rushed in, I cried out to him running into his arms as he walked in, "Dave, I don't think she's going to make it this time."

I tried to calm down but found it difficult because of her obvious struggle for each breath. There I sat, staring at her, holding on to Dave's hand with my right hand and Dawn's with my left so she knew we were there with her.

At 6:00 p.m., Dave went down the hall to smoke his pipe. When he came back, he said that Shelly wasn't in her room. I cried out, "Oh no, she must have died."

Dave said, "Maybe she had to go for X-rays or something."

"Oh no," I said, "she hasn't been out of her room for weeks."

When Becky came in to check Dawn, I asked her about Shelly. She confirmed that Shelly died about 4:00 p.m. I had noticed that when Becky came into Dawn's room earlier she looked upset as if she had been crying. Then I knew why.

Hearing about Shelly's passing left me feeling very sick. Dawn had been in the room next to Shelly's for two weeks. Even though I had never talked with her, I had heard her cries of pain. I talked to her mother several times about the situation both of us were in, with regard to our daughters. I could tell, by these talks, that Shelly's mom had a strong faith and was much better prepared to give up her daughter than I was.

My heart told me I should be ready to turn her over to God, but my mind said, *Please, God, let her stay here with me. I'll take care of her.*

A little after 7:00 p.m., friends from work stopped by to see me. They urged me to go with them a few minutes for coffee. I decided to go. Dave promised he'd come and get me if there was any change.

We had no more than sat down with our coffee when I saw my friend Maryann, who had been in Dawn's room, appear in the doorway. Panic hit; I jumped up and asked, "Is something wrong with Dawn?"

She said, "You'd better come right away." I raced up the two flights of stairs to get to Dawn's room. I was out of breath when I got to her bedside. As I looked at her pale, limp body, I screamed at Dave, "She's gone?"

"No, she's not," he said. "She's in between breaths."

Just then she took a long but very shallow breath. I held her hand, crying, "Please don't leave me, Dawn. I need you so much."

After four more very shallow breaths, Dawn left this world to be with Jesus. She struggled right up to the end, which had been her style for the last seven and a half years. When I realized her breathing had stopped, I heard Becky say, "I'm sorry, Mrs. Smith, but she's gone now."

I laid my head on Dawn's chest, still hanging on to her hand with Dave hanging on to me. I cried hysterically not wanting to let go. Others in the room just stood crying not knowing what to say. Dave kept saying, "She's safe with Jesus now."

I was finally able to say, "I'm not crying for Dawn. I'm crying for myself. I'm going to miss her very much."

While I was crying, Lori and my niece Tammy walked into the room, not knowing what had happened. When I saw Lori, I cried out, "Lori, your sister is gone."

"Oh, no," she cried, realizing she had gotten there too late. I wanted to put my arms around Lori but couldn't pull myself away from Dawn. She turned to Tammy and then her Dad for comfort.

Eventually, Becky suggested we go to the nurses' conference room while she took out all Dawn's tubes. She said we could come back later.

The hospital's chaplain, Father Bill, came to be with us as did Dr. Bergman, the resident on Dawn's case this time. She had been a very supportive.

The nurses offered all of us coffee and Kleenex as we tried to pull ourselves together. Lori called her boyfriend, Mark, so he came to give her comfort. I knew what had just happened had to be accepted but wanted to believe it was just a bad dream. Father Bill stayed with us until our pastor, Reverend Peterson arrived.

We sat around, talking about Dawn's happiest times. Many people had been touched by her life and fighting spirit. The faith she gained during her struggles became noticeably strong.

Becky came in saying, "You can go back and see Dawn now." Dave, Lori, Mark, and I all went back to Dawn's room. After I looked at her and touched her, I wished I hadn't come back. Her face was white and her body cold. I looked at Dave and said, "She's not here anymore, let's go." I was sick to my stomach with a headache. Dave put his arms around my waist and walked me into the hallway. Lori had left with mark and DJ was not there at all that night. The nurses had already packed her things, so nothing looked the same.

When I left that room, I couldn't get out of the hospital fast enough. Before I got into the car, I looked up to the sky and said, "Dawn, you are now free of pain, safe in the arms of Jesus." All the way home I stared, wondering how I was going to get along without my little girl.

Upon arriving home, we found a box of groceries on the back steps. There was a pastor's card from a church I had never heard of. Feeling grateful, I couldn't help but think how God had been taking care of our family all through Dave's unemployment and my leave of absence. I felt God had been working through the hearts of our family and friends. They had been there for us during those rough times.

My family had heard the news of Dawn's passing, so started coming over to offer help and sympathy. Reverend Peterson also said prayers when he droped by with Dawn's things left at the hospital.

After everyone had gone and I was in bed, I started questioning God about why he was doing this to me. I didn't want to be another mother who had lost her child to cancer. I didn't feel strong enough to go through that process.

When a very restless night was over, I realized the cold fact that Dawn would never be in this house again. That thought hit me as though a ton of bricks had banged against my head.

Willie and Louie went with Dave and me to make funeral arrangements. As soon as we walked into the funeral parlor, the owner said, "You have my sympathy, but we knew it was going to happen, didn't we."

I thought, *What a cold statement!*

When we all walked into the room to pick out a casket, I fell apart. I just couldn't perceive putting Dawn into one. I left abruptly, leaving Dave to make the decision on which one to select.

On Sunday, when I walked into the funeral home, I took my first look at Dawn in the casket. It was too much. I wanted to run over and take her out of there. She looked like Sleeping Beauty, but she didn't belong in there. As I stood by her, tears streaming down my face, I said, "Dawn, you left me, and now you're with Jesus." I felt so cheated because I couldn't have her with me anymore.

Many family members, friends, and church family members came by to offer their sympathy. Dawn's friend from grade school came by. Her name is Dawn Marie Smith, just like my Dawn's. She walked in and said, "Hi, Mrs. Smith, I'm Dawn's friend, Dawn." I couldn't get over how grown up and nice looking she was. I hadn't seen her since she was a pudgy little girl. Now she stood tall and slim. My mind wandered off thinking how my Dawn would look if she had been able to grow and develop normally. D.J. spent a lot of time standing by Dawn but not showing any emotion. I wondered what he was thinking. I hadn't seen him cry since Dawn died. He'd been neglected so much the past seven years that I wondered if he felt relieved that it was over.

On Monday, August 23rd, we went to our United Methodist Church for Dawn's funeral service. I wanted it to be a testimony of her Christian life. Our pastor friend, Bill Doubblestein, took part in the service along with our pastor, Reverend Peterson.

I walked by Dawn's casket one last time. It upset me so much that I didn't hear much of the service. My mind kept wandering off to days when Dawn and I were together.

All the seats in the church were filled, which everyone said was a wonderful tribute to the kind of person she was. She was loved and would be missed by many people. Her vibrant spirit was a testimony to many people.

It wasn't until late that night, after Dave and I had gone to bed, that I heard the beautiful service that was held earlier. We had asked that the service be taped, because of the certainty that I'd be too upset to absorb it. Tears filled my eyes as I listened to the beautiful music sung by Cory, a young Christian man. The last statement made by our pastor, "Our treasures are in heaven, waiting for us someday," really stood out for me. Dawn was and is a treasure, and heaven is now her home. I pictured her waiting for me with open arms. In the weeks to follow, that tape became an important tool in my healing process.

The next day I found myself wandering around the house in a daze. All the people that had been around, giving me support, were now going on with their own lives. Now, I had to figure how to go on with mine without Dawn to care for.

I looked through the book that people had signed when they came to the funeral home. I was amazed at the number of people who had signed it. Even Robert Woodrick, president of D&W, sent me a letter before Dawn died. For a week after Dawn's passing, we received many cards in the mail. D.J. and Lori liked to go after the mail and bring me all the cards. The cards with messages of concern written on them helped me get through those first lonely days.

Dave and I were taken by surprise when a couple from our church came over with a love gift from the congregation. It was such a generous amount. We received a love gift from the men's and women's group also. The prayers, love and monetary gifts showed us that God truly uses Christians to spread His love.

Besides our church family, there were other people in the community who expressed their concern for our family through gifts of money. Living in a small city, many people knew of Dawn's long illness, Dave's unemployment, and then my leave from work. It was a great comfort to know that, even though I felt alone sometimes, others shared our problems and wanted to help.

While trying to pull myself back together, I found it hard to carry on a conversation with people. They wanted to avoid mentioning Dawn's name, while she was nearly all I could think about. Every time I saw one of her possessions, I'd cry. Walking into her room and seeing her clothes hurt the most. My thought was, *Dawn won't ever wear these again.* That thought was just too much to bear and caused me to get myself worked up many times. The memories of our times together came flooding back.

Two weeks after Dawn's passing, I was still crying most of the time and feeling lost and empty. Lori and D.J. were so busy with their lives that they were seldom home. They didn't need me the same way Dawn did.

One day I had a wild crying spell because of taking care of Dawn's nightgowns. Picking one up and holding it close, I cried out "Dawn, why did you have to leave me? I need you so much." Wanting some comfort, I went to Dave, expressing my hurt.

He held me and then said, "Marilyn, you have to pull yourself together. Dawn is with God now and not suffering." He had a stern tone in is voice stern, pushed me away and walked off.

I knew he was right, but I didn't feel he understood how much harder it was for me, than him, to accept that. Knowing she was better off didn't compensate for not having her there with me. I became very tired of hearing people say, "Isn't it a blessing that God took her?" I didn't think people realized that, even though Dawn was suffering, it was hard for me to consider her death as a blessing.

Feeling Dawn's spirit was important to me. One Sunday, after we had communion, I thought about her so much that I felt the need to write to her. I sat down and wrote a poem to her.

Dawn

Your pass through life was but seventeen years,
While memory of you leaves me with many tears.
Through pain, you fought for seven years to keep your home with me.
With tears, I saw you sinking from what I thought you'd be.
My heart is truly broken though you fought so hard to stay.
You've finished the course of this life, while keeping faith each day.
Yes, you've spoken with firm certainty as to how your life relates.
So now you've passed with pleasure through those heavenly, pearly gates. Your memory is a keepsake with which I'll never part.
God has you in his keeping, and I have you in my heart.
Your new home is now in heaven, but I see you as you were.
I'll keep the faith, as you did, and will someday meet you there.

In loving memory, Mom

Besides the need to write her, I often walk by Dawn's picture on the wall stopping to talk. I see her beautiful blue eyes that were so expressive. It's just another one of my ways to keep her close.

In September, I went back to work, hoping to get my mind on things other than my sorrow. I found that my fellow workers, along with my regular customers, were at a loss for words. They felt uncomfortable, not knowing what to say. I felt uncomfortable, because I knew they were. It took a while before they would carry on a normal conversation. I found they were afraid that if Dawn's name was mentioned it would be too painful for me. On the contrary, I wanted her name to be mentioned, so I would feel free to express my feelings.

Another problem that came up was my feeling toward mothers and their children. Every time I saw a lady with a little girl, I recalled Dawn's childhood, thinking to myself, *Will that mother get to see her daughter grow up? I had a happy, healthy little girl at one time, too.* It was difficult not to feel cheated every time I'd see a mother and teenage daughter. I liked to think about how Dawn would have looked had she been given the chance to have a normal life.

Even though I could watch Lori and D.J. grow and develop, it didn't seem to fill the void in my life. My depression seemed to get worse as the weeks went on. Dave and I started fighting over the least little thing.

I felt Dave, Lori, and D.J. would deliberately change the subject every time I'd bring up Dawn's name. They didn't feel the need to keep Dawn's memory constantly in mind like I did. This I resented, feeling they should miss her as much as I still do.

On the days I'd come home from work with pain in my leg, I picked on Lori and D.J. the minute I walked in. Dave told me to quit taking my frustrations out on them, but I didn't realize I was doing that. I thought they didn't understand the physical and mental pain I was going through. Those days I missed Dawn even more and hated the world because I felt so miserable.

I kept praying to God to give me new strength and purpose in my life. My feeling was that He would bring something; it was not knowing what or when that was depressing.

With Dawn on my mind so much, I wanted to do something for the nurses at Butterworth Hospital and Dr. Gracias. They were a part of her life for many years.

Not knowing what kind of gift would be appropriate, I decided to express my gratitude in a poem.

I wrote a short poem to the nurses and had it put on a plaque. They were so happy I was able to express my feelings that they found a home for it on a wall of the pediatrics floor.

After giving the plaque to the nurses, I started working on a poem for Dr. Gracias. I wanted to put a lot of thought into it, because Dawn had so much faith in him. I wanted to express her feelings as well as mine. After spending much time and thought, I wrote the following.

Dr. Gracias

We've known you now for seven years.
You doctored all our needs.
You've been a friend when needed,
Especially to our Dawn.
Dawn's illness was a serious one
For which you did your part
To save her from a life of pain
From which she could not part.
Dawn's trust in you was justified
By your gentle, friendly way.
The faith and love she gained from
You is in our hearts to stay.
Our hopes and dreams, our plans for
Dawn, we've had to set aside.
God had a better plan for her
'Twas not the same as thine.
We thank you, Dr. Gracias, for
All that you have given.

You shared with us a precious life
Which God's now taken to Heaven.
With thankfulness,
Dave and Marilyn Smith

When I finished the poem, I put it in a wooden frame, hoping to find a good way to present it to him. The opportunity came when Dave had to go to Butterworth Hospital in November for surgery on his broken leg that did not heal right straight, which left him with a bad limp. We found a doctor who said he could straighten it with surgery.

I let Dr. Gracias's nurse, Meridell, know that Dave was going to be in the hospital and that I wanted to give Dr. Gracias the poem. She set up a time that she thought he could come to see us.

Dr. Gracias came into Dave's room to say hi and used the opportunity to give him the poem. I was so moved to see the look on his face as he smiled and looked chocked up when he saw the poem, which had Dawn's picture on it.

He looked at Dave and me when he had finished reading it. With tears in his eyes, he said, "Thank you for such a nice gift. I loved Dawn as much as I love my own kids."

Quickly I said, "I know you did. I wanted to express my feelings to you for those years you gave so much to help her."

"Dawn will always be special to me," he said, trying to control his emotions. He then quickly left.

I found out later that he took the poem and shared his feelings about our family with another doctor.

The poem ended up in Dr. Gracias's office where he said he often looks at it and thinks about the courage Dawn showed in dealing with her illness.

In October, a pastor came to our church and talked about a mission trip to Haiti, which he'd be leading in February. He showed slides of sick children in Grace Children's Hospital there.

The purpose of the mission trip was to work at the hospital in several different capacities.

He told how the children at the hospital pour out their love to the workers, because they are starved for attention and love. The idea of helping at that hospital and receiving the love from those children really appealed to me.

As I left church, I felt God had spoken to me about going to Haiti. When I asked Dave about it, he said, "I think it's a great idea. It might be just the thing you need." I was really surprised at his answer, because I had never left him and the kids before. If I went on the trip, I'd be gone for two weeks.

At first, I had a hard time trying to make the decision about going. Leaving the country sounded scary. Once I made the commitment to go, I started getting excited.

I became so caught up in the Haiti trip that I felt happy again. Since Dawn loved kids and wanted to be a nurse, I felt she would be extremely happy to know I was going to be a volunteer in a children's hospital. Knowing that she'd want me to go helped me feel her spirit.

As the Christmas season came upon us, I found myself going deeper into my depression. I didn't want to go Christmas shopping or have anything to do with Christmas activities. I could only think about how much I missed Dawn. It didn't seem right to delve into this joyous season with a family member missing.

Having no happy spirit, I was glad when Christmas was over this past year. I let the real reason we celebrate Christmas be forgotten. It showed me that even though I call myself a Christian, I was thinking about my sorrow on Christmas, instead of the fact that God had given Christ to us on that day. Instead of drowning myself in pity, I should have at least been thankful for God's gift.

Once the holiday season was over, I started thinking more about my upcoming trip to Haiti. Dave was happy about my going on the trip, hoping it would help me turn my life around.

Dave and Lori took me to the airport on February 3rd, and waited until I boarded the plane for Haiti. I had mixed feelings when I kissed them good-bye, thinking about the difficult and emotional times we had just gone through. I wanted them to miss me, hoping they would be more understanding of my needs when I came back. It didn't seem that Dave was giving me enough emotional support. He didn't want me to bring up Dawn's name around Lori and D.J., as if we should forget her now that she was with God. So much of my time revolved around Dawn when she was sick that Lori and D. J. probably felt neglected. I felt they wanted me to forget about Dawn and turn my attention completely on them. I wished they were now at a young age, where I could be more involved. Lori, at nineteen, has a steady boyfriend, while D.J., at thirteen, has sports activities on his mind. Dawn needed much motherly cuddling, which I miss giving.

My first impression of Haiti as I walked off the plane that night was, "Oh, what a terrible smell." We were told Haiti has a distinct smell because so many of the people use charcoal to cook with.

I spent two weeks in Haiti with twenty other people from the United Methodist Church. We went to work at Grace Children's Hospital, which houses children stricken with malnutrition and tuberculosis.

The first time I walked into the large, one-hundred-bed room where the children stay, it was heartbreaking. Many of the children have bloated bellies and skinny frames, evidence of malnourished bodies. Others lie sick and crying. As we walked about the room, the healthier children rushed to us, wanting our attention. I found that picking up one child led to picking up three more. They hugged me like I've never been hugged before.

I was so touched by these children that I found it hard to leave them at the end of each visit. They didn't make it easy, because as we'd leave, they'd hang on to us, crying hysterically.

Each time I visited the children, I felt Dawn's spirit. Every hug I received was like receiving one from her, since she loved kids so much. I felt Dawn was looking down at me saying, "Mom, those kids need you. Love them."

Haitian kids from the streets hung around the front gate of our hotel. They were always asking for food and clothes. We also had a lot of peddlers selling their wares. Each time we walked out to the gate, they'd be there. During the course of the two weeks, we got to know the kids and peddlers quite well. We called them our "gate family."

One child, a ten-year-old boy, really captured my heart. He couldn't speak any English, but he did learn to speak my name. Every time he smiled and hugged me, I melted.

One thing he kept begging for was sneakers. The shoes he wore were so small the heels had to be cut out.

I got to know the boy named "Bebe" so well that before I left I wanted him to have a new pair of shoes. As it turned out, a man staying at our hotel, who often comes to Haiti bringing clothes and shoes, gave me a pair of sneakers that fit Bebe.

Two others from our group and I presented Bebe with the new shoes. He was so happy that every time he came to our hotel after that he'd smile, pointing to his shoes. It felt good to see Bebe so happy just because of a pair of shoes.

While in Haiti, we visited several mission projects that our church helps to sponsor. The culture of Haiti was quite a shock. I haven't done enough traveling to see how other people live, so this trip had quite an affect on me.

The night before we left, I had very mixed emotions. I wanted to go home where I understood the language and where I could get fresh water out of a faucet, but I liked being there where I felt loved and useful.

I had been so busy being involved with the people of Haiti that I hadn't missed my family and felt very guilty about that. The only person I'd thought about was Dawn. I thought about her because I knew she had suffered like the kids in Haiti. I also thought about her because I knew she would be missing from the family that met me at the airport when I returned.

When Dave and I returned from our trip to Hawaii, all three of our children were at the airport waiting for us with open arms. I kept running that scene through my mind. The idea of Dawn not being there was so depressing.

The final morning when my new friend Mary and I walked out to the plane, we heard someone calling my name. I turned around and saw Bebe standing on the concourse. He was waving his arm, yelling, "Marilyn, Marilyn." Mary and I waved back and threw him a kiss. As we continued to the plane, we started crying. Minutes later, as we sat in our seats, we continued crying. We could still see Bebe standing there waving his arm.

We asked ourselves, *Why are we crying? We should be glad to be leaving this poverty-stricken country. We're going home where life isn't a struggle for us.* We knew why we were crying. We knew that we had learned to love the people and felt good about the work we did here.

I left not knowing what would happen to this young boy, Bebe, who I'd learned to love like my own. I didn't feel good knowing that he didn't have parents to love him and care for his needs. I knew there were lots of kids like him in Haiti, but I hadn't met them, and that made it easier to forget once I got home.

When I walked off the plane, my mom, dad, Dave, Lori, and D.J. were all there to greet me. I was happy to see them, but my mind drifted off to Dawn. *Why wasn't she there?* This family was not complete without her. By the time I greeted everyone with a kiss, I was crying because Dawn couldn't be with us.

I was excited with everything about my trip, even bringing home souvenirs bought from Haitian peddlers. I learned so much, that I spent the next few days talking about it to everyone.

Even though I didn't realize it at first, the Haitian trip turned my life around. Many churches and organized groups were interested in learning more about Haiti. I took movies while there, so I was able to put together a program. I spent a lot of time the next few months speaking in front of church and other groups.

I'd never gotten up in front of people and talked before, so I felt good that I was able to do that. I felt God had given me confidence in myself to speak in front of people, because He wanted me to tell about the work being done in Haiti.

Working at Grace Children's Hospital in Haiti was so rewarding that I decided to work as a volunteer at Butterworth Hospital. The Haiti experience helped me realize how useful one can be. I felt Dawn's spirit in Haiti probably because she would be happy to know that I was helping sick children. I wanted to feel that same spirit again. Feeling close to her is important to me.

Losing a child is a very devastating experience, but I have found that with God's love, a parent can overcome it and go on. Drowning oneself in pity serves no use and does not bring back the child. With God's help, I want to go on with life and do some of the things that would make Dawn proud of me.

I've discovered that being a volunteer can be one of the most rewarding experiences in life.

I don't feel God chose me to go through seven years of heartache, but because I did, He helped me get through it. I've become close to God by reading His Word daily and asking for guidance. Because of learning so much through these experiences, I feel it has made me a better person and much more sensitive to people's needs. I want to be a better disciple for God's work.

There are still days that bring depression and the feeling of great loss. When one comes, I walk by Dawn's picture and look at those beautiful, expressive eyes. Then I try to concentrate on the seventeen years I had with her and be thankful. Even with the pain of giving her up to God, I'd rather have had her for a short time than not to have had her at all.

Losing a son or daughter has to rank as one of the most traumatic experiences a loving parent has to endure. Although parents react to such tragedies differently, each one feels the loss of a part of his or her own life.

The poem my brother-in-law, Wally, wrote back in 1976 has meant a lot to me through the years. Because it means so much, I have rewritten it to express my feelings of what Dawn's life means to me now.

Dawn

Dawn was the glimmering hope of a brand new day.
Dawn's shining existence made the darkness slip away.
Dawn's presence in summer caused birds to sing.
Dawn shed light and loveliness on everything.
Dawn began a warmth that lasted the whole day through.
Dawn relieved the hard nights, for she had been there too.
Dawn was a daughter to me, not the rising sun.
Dawn, like the sun, gave strength and hope to everyone.
Dawn's life was a vibrant witness to a living God above.
Dawn in every way was within the power of His love. So when this proud old Mom feels all hope is gone, All she has to do, is remember the shining eyes of Dawn.

Dealing with Dawn's seven years of illness and then death has been an up-and- down-hill emotional battle. It put stress on Dave's and my marriage and my relationship with Lori and D. J. Many times I've felt that we couldn't handle any more, but then we did. As each new problem came up, we somehow handled it.

Keeping God at the center of our lives has been the answer. God has given us a church with caring people to love and uplift us during crises. God has also given us Scripture to reassure us of His love. God doesn't exempt Christians from life's problems, but He promises to help us get through them. Dawn's suffering is over, but the rest of us must go on and face life's struggles. I face my own struggle with the physical pain I confront daily. Because of the faith I've gained, I now deal with it differently. In my reading of Scripture, I prefer to use *The Living Bible* translation. I turn to it frequently, particularly when in need of receiving renewed strength.

The scripture that I constantly go back to for strength is Romans 5: 3-5:

> We can rejoice, too, when we run into problems and trials for we know that they are good for us they help us learn to be patient. And patience develops strength of character in us and helps us trust God more each time we use it until finally our hope and faith are strong and steady. Then, when that happens, we are able to hold our heads high no matter what happens, and know that all is well, for we know how dearly God loves us, and we feel this warm love everywhere within us because God has given us the Holy Spirit to fill our heart.